MW00328864

PROJECT VANLIFE

"The adventure these two young people shared is amazing... The perseverance they exhibited was awe inspiring."
- Sandi Christman

"An encouraging read for those who dream big and work hard to make those dreams a reality, this story of the epic summer road trip entertains and offers insight into the lives of individuals driven to succeed."
- Kevin Joell

"Not content to color within the lines, Trevor and Sierra set out on a cross country road trip and realize how their University education relates to real life and to living their dream of being entrepreneurs."
- Dagmar Bohlmann

PROJECT VANLIFE

This book is based on a true story. No part of this book shall be reproduced in any way without written consent of the authors. The exception would be in the case of brief quotations where proper credit is given.

Copyright © 2014 by Trevor DeRuisé and Sierra Davies.
All rights reserved.

Originally published in paperback by Blü World Inspired Publishing, Reno, Nevada in 2014.

Printed in the United States of America

ISBN: 978-0692318430

Book design and text composition by Blü World Inspired.

PROJECT VANLIFE

Trevor DeRuisé
Sierra Davies

BLüWORLD
INSPIRED

The Bigger Picture

Fueled by Passion & Driven by Adventure - Trevor

"I've got to get out of here," I think to myself in a groggy daze.

Panic begins to set in as I become more awake and alert. The air is hot. Unnaturally hot. It's also thick and moist, providing the sensation of drowning.

"I've got to get out of here!" my mind now screams at the rest of my half-sleeping body.

I stagger to my knees. Peeling my clammy flesh off the rubber air mattress beneath me creates a sound and feeling similar to the removal of an old Band-Aid.

Still kneeling, I sloppily yank open the door of my 2004 Ford Econoline van and scramble outside to be greeted by a slightly cooler but still thick and damp breeze. The hot but moving air is liberating in contrast to the dungeon I had just escaped.

Gravel cuts into my bare feet as a herd of eighteen-wheelers idles in the distance. I squint and try to make out the words on the sign at the end of the gravel lot as the sun burns my tired eyes. "$2.99 All You Can Eat," I think it says. My panic slowly washes away with the waves of questions that begin to flood my brain. The most pertinent of these concerns my location.

Where was I? Idaho? No, that was five nights ago. Wyoming? No, that was three nights ago. Colorado? No mountains, so this can't be Colorado. But what was after Colorado? Ah, that's right... Kansas.

As I assess the situation in the parking lot of what must be a truck stop in what I am about 80 percent sure was Kansas, Sierra jumps out of the van with the exact same, panicked, "I've got to get out of

2

here!" look that I had just moments ago. She doesn't say anything, and I watch as her mind processes the same information I had just assembled. The expression on her face slowly evolves from terror to dull understanding as she looks at me and asks, "Kansas?"

This was how Sierra and I started each day for nearly three months, give or take a few details. Every single morning around 6:00 a.m. the sun pierced the side of our van, turning it into some kind of lethal Easy Bake Oven. Combine this with the thick and humid air of Mid and Eastern North America and you've got quite the recipe for an abrupt and unpleasant wake-up call. Who needs an alarm clock when Mother Nature turns your bedroom into a sauna at the same time each morning? Besides, alarm clocks require electricity – a luxury not available to those living in a used cargo van.

Once awake, the next hour or so would be dedicated to putting the pieces back together of the extremely scattered puzzle that was our life. *Where were we? Did we have food? What's on the training plan today? What's on the travel itinerary?* These were the kinds of questions that crafted our tight schedule every day.

Surely, when people see two college-aged kids evacuate a van in the morning with no shoes and seemingly no comprehension of their surroundings, assumptions are going to be made about their objectives in life and overall contribution to society. But this, I assure you, is not something Sierra and I are strangers to, nor is it something we lose sleep over.

Our agenda on a daily basis seemed to fight with the constraints provided by the speed of the revolving earth. Twenty-four hours just isn't enough. It hasn't been enough for as long as I can remember. Why? Because this world has way too many incredible things to build, people to inspire, places to visit, and goals to accomplish to be limited to twenty-four short hours each day.

This was no leisurely road trip we set out on. We were chasing the Pro Cross-Country Tour, the premier professional mountain bike series in North America. The journey was scheduled to last over ninety days and take us well over 15,000 miles across this beautiful (and sometimes not-so-beautiful) continent, from coast-to-coast and everywhere in between.

The life Sierra and I have chosen is slightly different than the typical twenty-something-year-old college student. Saying we take "the road less traveled" would be a cliché and an immensely understated fallacy. We are on more of a "*trail* not yet traveled."

Hippies? Gypsies? Vagabonds? Sure, this snapshot of our lives holds more parallels with these varieties of people than I hope any other time in our future does. The one key and defining difference that we have been able to cling to through all of the struggles, though, is ambition.

It was the pursuit of our dreams that led us to this seemingly all-time low and relentless fight on a daily basis. It was also this pursuit that kept us joyful, hopeful, and inspired through whatever the wild journey threw our way. So don't be fooled by our self-inflicted hardship – we were actually having the time of our lives.

My name is Trevor DeRuisé and I am a 22-year-old professional mountain bike racer. Sierra? She's my girlfriend and the creative drive behind just about everything we do in this wild life we live together.

The summer of 2014 will forever symbolize our definition of the pursuit of happiness. It was proof that the American Dream *does* still exist; it has just taken on a slightly different form. Rather than white picket fences and working your way up the corporate ladder, our definition of the American Dream consists of a free, bold, and passionate life dedicated to something bigger than oneself. Our definition can be best illustrated through the life-altering endeavor that we refer to as *Project VanLife*.

The underlying themes and motives behind what was absolutely the adventure of a lifetime are ones that, tragically, are not taught in our education system here in America. In order to craft a career and a living out of your dreams and passions in life, you need a unique set of skills and ideals that no textbook can provide. Throughout this story, we hope to illustrate these so that you can take them along on your own endeavors.

Rather than hanging out and enjoying the relaxing, sunny days in between spring and fall semesters of college, Sierra and I went after something bigger. I would even go as far as saying that we went after something *huge*. We packed up my 2004 Ford Econoline van that I had acquired just a few months prior to our departure and we took to the road.

Living the glamorous life of a professional athlete, a trip like this should be a breeze, right? Surely, my sponsors would pave the way and foot the bill so all I would have to do is drive the van and pedal my bike. Unfortunately, this could not be farther from the reality. Our efforts would be the epitome of "grassroots" and bring us to the edge of calling the whole thing off numerous times as hardships and setbacks built up to unbearable levels.

On top of that, Sierra and I have a long list of extra curricular activities back home in the Reno-Tahoe area that we would have to take along with us. Running our business endeavors, non-profit organizations, planning for school, keeping up with sponsor obligations, and handling everything else that our tangled but passion-driven lives entail was tough enough. Doing it from the confines of our small, rolling headquarters with no Wi-Fi would be nearly impossible on top of our already ridiculous circumstances.

The goal of all of this? Well, the goal is slightly complicated. One would assume the purpose here would be to make it as a top professional mountain bike racer and live happily ever after. If only it were that simple...

I'd be lying if I said being the best mountain bike racer in the world isn't something I dream about. I want to be the best and I won't stop until I am. But the big picture for Sierra and me is so much more than that.

We're after a life fueled by passion and driven by adventure. We want to take the things we love in this world and turn them into lucrative careers that we can zealously build every single day we're

on this earth. We want to contribute to society while simultaneously inspiring others to step outside of their comfort zones and
take on passionate endeavors of their own, no matter how big or
small. Ultimately, we want to light a fire in future generations to
live their dreams.

Work For It - Trevor

I have always felt like I was dealt a pretty neutral hand when it comes to my life. While nothing has ever been handed to me, I've never viewed anything as exceptionally out of reach either. I think a lot of this can be attributed to perspective, rather than my actual circumstances.

Growing up, my mom worked part-time at a drug store, spending most of her day with my sister and me. My dad was an elevator technician who left early in the morning and usually didn't come home until late at night.

I was never the kid with the fancy new toy or the one throwing wild birthday parties at the local water park. At the same time, I never really wanted to be that kid. The only things I cared about paying for were dirt bike parts, which was often tough. I would never say that we were poor, but we were certainly humble.

While our modest situation can mostly be attributed to my dad's incredible financial discipline and ability to plan for the future (one of the many things I was less than fond of at the age of seven, but deeply admire now), it can also be attributed to the fact that my parents were doing it on their own. Money does not run deep in the blood of my family. Every single thing my parents have today is a result of nothing but their own hard work.

I have always tremendously admired my parents despite the fact that the path I have chosen for my life is very different than what they are accustomed to.

With my mom, her wit and ability to love always fascinated me. You'd never know whether we were going to the grocery store or to Disney Land with her because the level of spunk was always the same. Similarly, whether I had just gotten suspended from school or made it onto the Dean's List, she was always the first person I would go to. Partly because I wanted someone on my side when bad news made its way to my father, but also just because I knew whatever was going on, good or bad, she had my back.

With my dad, it is undoubtedly his work ethic that I admire most. He's a man of few words and if I had a yacht for every time he's hugged me, I would still have zero yachts. But this wasn't his role in my life, and that has just always been understood between us. To my dad, a hug was staying up all night to fix my broken bike so I could race the next day. A hug was leaving work an hour early on Friday and then driving twenty hours straight so that I could race on Saturday. Once the checkered flag would fall, he would load my bike up and drive twenty hours back home so he didn't miss work on Monday.

This is how my dad showed his affection and at the same time taught me what would become the most valuable lesson I've ever learned and the driving factor in all of my endeavors today. He taught me that if you want *anything* in this world, you have to work for it. Even more, he taught me to *never* quit.

This was tough for me to grasp as a kid and it wasn't until much later in my life that it really began to dictate my actions.

Learn From Defeat - Trevor

I haven't always raced bicycles. In fact, there was a time when I *swore* I would never wear any of that silly spandex I'd see cyclists wearing on the side of the road as we'd drive by in our big diesel truck on the way to the moto track. Motorcycles were, and in most ways still are, my entire world.

When I was little I loved sports and hated school. Unfortunately for me, but to my parents' delight, my talents were the other way around. I could get A's without touching a book all the way through college, but I was hands down the worst kid on the tee ball field everywhere we went. I would trip over the soccer ball, could not hit the backboard with a basketball to save my life, and I even took a whack at tennis but never succeeded in making that "whack" come in contact with that dreadful fuzzy sphere. As the other kids would often say, I sucked. All of these athletic calamities took place over the course of about a year. Then, when I was five, everything changed the day my dad took me to my first motorcycle race to spectate.

It was a small, local event, taking place inside of the convention center in downtown Reno. I'll never forget that night and the impact it had on my life. The allure of the race tugged at every single one of my senses. The smell of burning race gas; the rumble as the gate dropped and twenty bikes roared into the first turn; the breathtaking sight of a man and a bike flying eighty feet through the air over the finish line jump – I was hooked.

At just five years of age I begged my parents for a motorcycle. I had a bicycle, which I was a self-proclaimed 'shredder' on, but you can't jump a bicycle like they did on motorcycles. To my knowledge, you couldn't even race a bicycle, but you could race a motorcycle.

My parents were not exactly keen on the idea of getting me a motorcycle. I had it at the top of my Christmas list for almost six months, but they were persistent with their stance on the matter.

Disappointed and thinking about which "ball sport" I would try next, I tried to let the whole idea go. But then it happened. Christmas morning rolled around and there it was. My very first, shiny, orange, and brand-new motorcycle was sitting in our living room. It was a KTM, 50cc bike, which I immediately fell in love with.

My dad took me riding for the first time later that day, and it was everything I had anticipated it would be and more. Still to this day, I can say there is nothing on this planet that I love more than the thrills you can experience while atop two wheels. As cliché as it may sound, the freedom and joy a bike provides is unlike anything else. I felt as though I could go anywhere and do anything, as long as I had my bike.

Later that year, I got into racing and for the first time an athletic activity clicked with me. Finally, I had a sport where I felt like I could actually compete with everyone else. Even as a kid, I often wondered if I excelled at riding bikes by chance, or if it was because I actually cared about it. I can honestly say I didn't like any of those "ball sports." I tried them all because my friends played them.

I was so drawn to the glory that would rain down on a baseball player on TV after he hit a home run or after a basketball player made the final shot just before the buzzer and won the game. There was a thrill to the kind of competition that sport provided that I just couldn't imagine finding anywhere else besides on a field or court. I wanted that but I had blindly sought after it down a path that I despised.

I dreaded going to soccer practice, but would beg my dad to take me riding. When I started racing I never once thought of riding as "practice," even though that's exactly what it was. As things got more serious and my dad would work with me on different skills, techniques, and types of terrain, it was still just riding to me, and there was nothing else in the world I would rather do.

I won my first championship just a year later at the age of six and that was it. At that moment, I knew what I wanted to do with the rest of my life. I knew what my passion was in this world and what I would be content doing for the rest of my life.

Of course, I was only six, so what did I know? Every kid wants to be a racecar driver, astronaut, or rock star when they grow up, right? I think the difference was that I actually experienced it. I actually got a small glimpse into the life of a motorcycle racer. I had felt the agony of defeat time and time again in every sport I had tried and finally triumphed and tasted victory. It's a feeling I've only experienced a few times in life, most of which would again come from success atop a bike.

What's more, I had gotten so fed up with the things other kids would say to me after my umpteenth air ball or strike out that failure no longer scared me. There was nothing you could say to me that I hadn't already heard or that hadn't already crossed my mind. I think learning just how powerless the negative opinions of others can be from a young age is extremely valuable. *Haters gon' hate*, and that should never be a deterrent from living the life of your dreams.

Despite whatever doubt or criticism I faced, I knew I wanted to race bikes for a living and nothing was going to stop me. To this day, I'm still not really sure how my parents took this. They were very neutral in their approach to my racing, which I think is what created such a deep hunger within me for the sport. While top racers my age were usually pulled out of school so they could train and race full time, my time on the bike was limited to my dad's work schedule. This made every second at the track so much more precious. While burnout began to strike several of my competitors, my fire was just getting started.

As the years went by, I started winning more and more. I would beg my dad to take me riding every weekend and late in the evening on the weekdays after he got home from work.

When I started high school, the big picture started to form in my mind. I began to realize that it didn't matter how badly I crushed a local or regional race. I needed to think bigger. I needed to get outside of Nevada and start chasing national level events if I ever wanted to make something of my racing.

Several local guys I knew of who had landed themselves rides with elite teams from racing a series called the World Off Road Championship Series, or WORCS. The races took place across the country and attracted all of the top manufacturers and teams. I knew it would be a stretch, but I ran the idea of chasing such an enormous series by my dad.

At first, it didn't seem like a very promising notion, but I stayed persistent with my campaign. For almost a year, I bugged my dad on a daily basis regarding the WORCS series. I would Google all of the driving routes to the races and think up ridiculous scenarios of driving all night long so that we could make it to far-away races and back in a weekend so that he didn't have to miss a day of work.

My dad is a mysterious man who rarely answers questions directly, so I really had no idea if any of my antics were helping or not. Every time I would provide him a reason why we should make an effort to contest these races, he wouldn't say "yes" or "no." Instead, he would simply provide me a reason as to why we could not do them. Every time he would do this, I took it as a challenge and I'd spend the next week working up a solution to bring back to him, as well as another reason as to why we *should*. This quite literally went on all the way through summer and into winter.

When December rolled around, it was game time in my eyes. The first WORCS race was in Arizona in mid January and I wanted to be there.

I was fifteen years old at the time when Christmas came around that year. Rather than opening gifts and rejoicing in the assortment of objects I had just acquired, I got something so much better.

"You want to go to Arizona next month?" my dad casually asked.

That was it. That was all I needed. That was my dad's way of telling me we were about to take on one of the biggest endeavors of our lives together.

I started working everywhere I could to save up money to help pay for motorcycle parts and entry fees. I took a job with my grandfather, roofing houses in the blazing Nevada heat the previous summer. I took a job at the mall, selling shoes. I mowed lawns all up and down our neighborhood. I sold lemonade. I did everything I could, but I also learned that the more I worked, the less time I had to ride and train.

This is when I started to figure out time management and the value of an hour. If I worked at the mall and made $7.25 per hour, I had to account for the thirty-minute drive to and from my three-hour shift. When you do the math, I was making quite a bit less than the already minuscule hourly rate. So, working at minimum wage for ten hours per week, it would take me almost three weeks to pay for a single entry fee. Plus, I'd be left with almost no time to ride and actually prepare for these bigger races, especially when you factor in my school schedule.

I needed to do something different. I needed a way that I could work less, get paid more, and do it all on my own agenda. But it's important to remember, I was far from a money-hungry teen with the desire to get rich. Rather, I knew that doing things my own way was the only way I could accomplish my racing dreams.

It would be fair to say that this was my introduction to the world of entrepreneurship. While I was still far from being an entrepreneur, I began to form the mindset of an entrepreneur. I'll discuss this topic in much greater detail later on.

When the first race rolled around that January, words could not describe the emotions that were flooding through me. While I was ecstatic to have the opportunity to pursue this renowned series, I was also somewhat terrified of lining up against the top amateur talent in the country for the first time. Not to mention, we were on a very tight travel schedule, which consisted of one of the longest drives I had ever done from Reno, Nevada down to Phoenix, Arizona and back in the span of three days. Oh, and I had to race my motorcycle somewhere in between.

I won't go into the specifics of how the weekend went, but I will say that I got smoked. That's right, I got obliterated and I was only an amateur. It was one thing to swallow this on my own, but I had much more weighing on me. My dad had invested so much into the whole trip, my bike, and me and I blew it. I spent the next twenty hours sitting silently in the truck just thinking as we drove through the night and into the next morning to make it back in time for my dad to get to work and me to school.

At this point, I figured I had two options. The first was to call it quits. Before I wasted any more time or money from the people I love, just call the whole thing off and stick to the normal local racing scene which I already knew I could win at. Or, I could improve. I could rise to the occasion, learn from the beat down I had received in Phoenix, and come back swinging at Round 2.

Fortunately, for the sake of this book and for the sake of everything else I have going on in my life today, I chose the latter. I started to pick the entire experience in Arizona apart and figure out what went wrong. I determined some of the issues were simply logistical caused by our terrible travel schedule. However, I knew the majority of the issues were specific weak spots in my riding that I needed to work on. So, that is exactly what I did.

All of my friends were starting to get into the party scene during this time, but I chose not to indulge. Rather, Saturday and Sunday were dedicated to nothing but moto. I also worked out a more consistent schedule with my dad of weeknight riding when he got off work. Any free time was strictly dedicated to my self-tailored and ever-changing, yet undeniably rigorous training schedule.

I didn't know much about physical fitness, but I did know I needed more of it to be the best. Most people don't understand how physically demanding motocross can be. Sure, cruising around on a dirt road on a motorcycle does not take much fitness. However, pinning it out of a sandy turn and ramming over five-foot-deep whoops (mounds of dirt that form on motorcycle tracks due to bikes hitting them over and over again) at fifty miles per hour, just to slam on the brakes, turn, and do it all over again takes some serious power and endurance.

On top of this, you cannot lose focus. Even when every muscle in your body is screaming out for you to stop, you have to stay completely focused. One small mental lapse that leads to a tiny mistake can quite literally and tragically be lethal.

During a typical race, my heart rate would max out at 200-215 beats per minute and then average around 190 for the remaining fifty minutes of the race. How do I know this? Because I bought a heart rate monitor since one of the many physiology and kinesiology books that I read suggested it. I read everything that I thought *might* give me even the smallest edge.

Once I got my driver's license, I started taking my mom's car to the gym down the street at 4:30 a.m. every morning for spin class. It consisted of mostly pregnant women and moms trying to get that "summer bod" back up to par, but those gals could rip. I absolutely hated spin class, but I felt like it was extremely valuable to my fitness. Immediately following spinning, I would lift weights for an hour or so before I'd rush my mom's car back home so she could get to work and I could get to school.

There certainly was not much direction or focus to my training, but that did not mean it lacked intensity or discipline. Looking back, I am very grateful for this. *While direction and focus can be acquired through knowledge and experience, intensity and discipline are something you either have or don't have, and this all stems from having a dream and being willing to do anything to achieve it.*

There was not a miraculous leap of improvement at the next race that following February. To be honest, that entire season went without the appearance of any miracles. However, there was steady improvement at every single race, which kept my hope alive. As long as I was headed in the right direction, I was content with putting in any amount of work necessary to create the life I wanted.

I was fortunate enough to have yet another opportunity to chase the WORCS series the following year. This time, I had some better sponsors, a better bike, and an overall better program to follow based upon the wealth of knowledge and experience I had acquired from the season before. Even more, I had an even bigger fire burning inside of me to win one of these things. While I didn't blow everyone out of the water going into this new season, something definitely felt different.

Sure enough, at the second round, I went one-one on the day, winning both of my races against the same guys who had embarrassed me just a year before. To further cement my excitement, I knew the wins did not come by luck or chance. In both motos I found myself fairly buried in the pack after the start and had to work my way to the front. Once there, I was able to pull away effortlessly, as if I was riding on a different track than everyone else. I use this analogy because I remember thinking this same thing about my competitors while driving home from Phoenix that sad night after my first shameful WORCS race.

I consider this race to be one of the most momentous days of my life. On this day I realized I could do anything that I felt was worthwhile enough to put the work into.

Yes, I know what you are thinking right now. Did I really just say that the overused, worn-out, and hollow saying "you can do anything you put your mind to" was true? Sort of. You see, it is only true for a select few. No, not those with exceptional genetics or a heritage that can be traced back to British Royalty. Rather, it is true for those who are actually willing to put the work in to make it true. It is true for those who can ignore the endless doubt of everyone around them and relentlessly chase something. It is true for those who want something so bad that it consumes their very being, and who will go to any lengths to have it.

I also started to see the world around me change after this race. People who had never once talked to me were approaching me in the pits like we had been friends forever. With this, a new confidence began to form, but it was also a valuable lesson on success. People are funny when it comes to the accomplishments of others. In the words of Donald Glover, "everyone hates you 'til they love you." If you're on the way up, people's own insecurities will cause some animosity within them towards you. That is, until you reach a point that they consider out of reach. Once there, people will view you in a much more positive light, or at least pretend to. It's important to be wary of people who wanted nothing to do with you until you were successful, but it's also important to be understanding of this natural phenomenon, as it's a fairly common attribute of human nature.

I even saw changes in my dad. I think for the first time he got a small glimpse of what I had been chasing from the start. Perhaps he had always seen it, but after this moment, it was as if he began to believe that perhaps it was possible.

My winning streak continued over the next three races. I was on an incredible high that unfortunately would not last long. You see, there's a rule in the WORCS series that if your lap times are too much faster than your competitors, you get moved up to the next division. While my goal for the season was to win an amateur championship in the series that had wiped the floor with me just a year before, my lap times had other plans.

At my hometown WORCS event, about an hour north of Reno, I received the news. My lap times and results over the past four events had caught the attention of the officials and I was booted out of my championship hunt. I showed up to this race hoping to have the same success I was having at the preceding four events, but now everything had changed. I felt as though I had been thrown into a shark tank and the expression "sink or swim" didn't even begin to explain my new circumstances. Rather, I would have to swim *and* avoid being eaten by the best off road motorcycle racers North America had to offer.

I was now racing in the Pro Lites division, on the same track and starting in the same gates as the heroes I had looked up to since I was a kid. I had not even fathomed being here for at least a few more years. According to my lap times, I had the speed to be here. However, according to my conscience, equipment, and game plan, I was far from ready.

You can think of the Lites class as the Development League in the NBA. Rather than throwing us straight into the deep end with all of the heavy hitters in off road racing, we were able to ease into this higher level of racing. We raced smaller displacement engines and only were in competition against each other, rather than the factory-backed famous riders who shared the gates with us.

As an amateur, the day had actually been pretty simple. You had a single, short practice in the morning, followed by your races in the afternoon. There was plenty of time in between to further prep the bike, hydrate, and relax.

Now, my schedule completely changed. Races became a three-day affair, complete with a practice on Friday, a practice in the morning on Saturday quickly followed by two, hour-long qualifying races, and then a two-hour long main event on Sunday.

Oh, and did I mention pro sections? These were quite frankly the most terrifying things I had encountered in my young life and I remember showing up to every event before this day and thinking "Boy am I glad I don't have to ride *that*." Now? Now I had to ride *that*.

Pro sections were portions of the track reserved just for the pro race. Why were they reserved just for the pros? *Because they were gnarly.* They were different at every round, consisting of jumps over small lakes or lagoons, fifteen-foot-tall rock water falls you had to maneuver up, man-made obstacles like tractor tires or a series of logs, or an uphill or downhill that was so steep and treacherous you couldn't even walk it during course inspection. *These* were pro sections and if you want to make it through them in one piece, you had better be a pro.

My first Lites race was less than spectacular to put it gently. Sure, my closest friends and family were ecstatic about my first appearance in the big leagues. To me, this was just the first step of what was sure to be yet another *long* journey to the top with obstacles, both on and off the track, larger than I could even comprehend at the time. While this *was* the goal I had been chasing for so long, it came at such a terrible time.

When you think motorcycle racing, you typically do not think "teams." The individuality of the sport is one of the things I loved most. However, at the top level it quickly becomes a team sport. By signing with a good team, riders acquire bikes, mechanics, and even their paycheck, which is what makes racing motorcycles for a living possible. The best way to sign with a good team is to stand out as an amateur. *This* would prove to be the critical step that I missed out on due to my sudden and unexpected jump. My dad and I worked relentlessly for the remaining season and the following one trying to get back to the top.

To me, it was all about numbers and finding a balance that always seemed unattainable. My competition was riding almost every single day and it certainly showed on race day with their incredible speed and fitness. Now that I had my driver's license, this was actually possible for me to pull off around my high school class schedule. However, it wasn't quite as simple as that. This is where the math starts.

On a dirt bike, every single part has several numbers associated with it. These numbers include the amount of hours you can ride before the part needs to be replaced, how much it costs, as well as the time it takes to replace it. The sad reality was that these numbers were beginning to rule my life and change the way I saw the sport I once loved. I didn't have practice bikes or mechanics to take care of these things for me. These were luxuries reserved for the elite, which I now, ironically, was supposed to be part of. Every time my bike fired up, the numbers would fill my mind.

Piston: 60 hours - $160 - 5 hours of labor
Tires: 30 hours - $250 - 2 hours of labor
Clutch: 50 hours - $100 - 3 hours of labor
Suspension: 90 hours - $60 - 6 hours of labor

…And the list goes on. What was once my escape from the world was now one of the most stressful activities in my life. It was a constant battle of knowing that I needed to practice, but at the same time, I needed to stay off my bike to keep it fresh for race day.

I had a few, brief glimpses of promise in what would end up being my final year as a motorcycle racer during my senior year of high school. The most significant came in Payette, Idaho, where I led every single lap of the main event on Sunday, only to be passed on the last lap due to a slight miscalculation with fuel in my bike. Why did the miscalculation happen? Because my dad and I had never been to the sandy hills of Payette, Idaho before, nor had we heard anything about the location. We had no idea the terrain would be so taxing on my motor, causing me to burn more fuel than usual. The new two-hour main events were still new to us, and so were their affects on my bike. How could we have known?

While I still ended up second in Idaho and it is still my best finish as a Pro Lites racer to date, it was hard to swallow how the loss came about. Especially given the difference in prize money and bonuses between first and second place, which we certainly could have used to soothe my number-filled and dollar-worried mind.

This was just one of many lessons learned the hard way that year. The entire season was a struggle. I knew I had the speed to be a top contender at every race even with my limited resources, and Idaho was proof of that. It just seemed like I was always losing the battle with the numbers in my head.

I would try riding less throughout the week so my bike was in better condition come race day; then not have the fitness to keep charging during the entire two-hour main event.

I would try riding more throughout the week, only to lead a large portion of the race before something on my bike failed due to the extra riding.

I was becoming fed up. As a teenager, challenges and struggles this big can be overwhelming and really wear you down. My seemingly constant adversity on the racetrack, combined with several injuries throughout the season had changed me. For the first time in my life, I was burnt out.

Keep an Open Mind - Trevor

About the same time I really began to get serious with my motorcycle racing, I began to dabble in cycling. I assure you, though, I was by no means a "cyclist." To me, a bicycle was nothing more than another piece of gym equipment. It wasn't a sport; it was a tool.

I was turned on to cycling when I found out that all of the top motorcycle racers used road cycling to build their endurance and fitness. So if the guys who were beating me were doing it, I had to do it, too.

When I was sixteen, I found my mom's 1980's pink Schwinn road bike in the shed. The wheels were out of true, the brakes were sketchy at best, only a handful of the gears worked, and it had a steel frame that seemed to weigh almost as much as I did.

Rather than easing into cycling, I jumped in the same way I jump into most things in life – head first. I had two moto friends who had become pretty strong road cyclists for the same reason I was now going to give this pedaling stuff a try. When they heard I had a bike to ride, they were thrilled and immediately took me under their wings. They took me out for my very first ride one hot summer afternoon in Markleeville, California. If you are familiar with cycling, you've probably heard of Markleeville. The mountains surrounding it are the same ones 3-time Tour de France winner Greg Lemond used to train while crafting the most illustrious cycling career of any American in history.

My friends continued to warn me on the drive down that I needed to drink water, continue to eat while riding, and turn around if I felt too fatigued. All of this seemed ridiculous to me. I could battle with the best motorcycle racers in North America for two solid hours so this pedaling stuff was going to be *cake*. Food and water were not something you had during a dirt bike race, so they surely would not accompany me while I rode my bicycle. Silly spandex bicycle shorts? *I think I'll pass, guys.* My cargo shorts and tennis shoes would work just fine.

They told me the ride would consist of two huge climbs – up the face of a mountain, down the other side, and back up and over to the car. In total, it would be about forty miles with about 6,000 vertical feet of elevation gain. Yes, they warned me about this and I didn't bat an eye. Perhaps it got lost in the exhaust-filled haze between my ears or perhaps I was just arrogant. I was pretty confident, I had this cycling thing handled.

As we started the ride, we spent the first few miles stopping frequently to adjust my seat and shifters. The seat seemed way too high and the handlebars felt way too narrow and low. I was terribly uncomfortable, but refused to let my friends get away from me as we cruised up the front side of Monitor Pass on the way to the 8,300-foot summit.

I made it to the top only about a minute behind one of my friends and about a minute ahead of the other. They must have seen the agony in my eyes, because they just kept reminding me to "take it easy."

"Cycling is *easy!*" I would yell back at them trying not to let the pending doom inside of my body show.

The truth is, I was struggling from the moment we left the car. While they were using the front side of the mountain to warm up and ease into the ride, I was going for broke just to hold on. When we got to the top, I wasn't sure what would happen, but I knew there would be severe consequences if I dropped down the other side rather than just turning back right then. However, my pride just wouldn't let me turn back.

"I'm fine, let's go!" I yelled and then plummeted down the backside of the mountain at forty miles per hour. My bike got so wobbly at high speed due to the bent wheels, I still to this day get nervous on road descents. When we got to the bottom and started heading back up, I didn't make it a single mile before things started going very wrong for me. *Very* wrong.

My back began to completely lock up from being in the strange, new position for so long. On top of that, my legs were cooked and enthusiasm was quickly fading. I started to pull off to the side of the road and pretend as if I was doing things. At first, I pretended like I needed to make a quick restroom break. Next, I needed to adjust my seat a little more. Etc.

By the second mile, I no longer had the energy for these clever excuses. I told both of my friends to go ahead without me and that I would just meet them at the top.

Once they took off, I got off my bike and started walking. The pain in my back and legs was unlike anything I had ever felt before. I probably walked another half mile before my vision started to get blurry and I felt extremely cold.

I tried sitting down to maybe get some blood back into my head. I was quickly becoming delirious and could no longer remember where I was, what I was doing, or how to get back home. I probably sat down for five minutes before even that was too much work and I needed to lie down. Almost immediately after I put my Schwinn on its kickstand and set my head down on the hot gravel aside the highway, I fell asleep.

So there I was, lying face down in the dirt, passed out on the side of the road. My friends had warned me about all of the things I had done wrong which had led me to my demise, but I hadn't listened. I was now experiencing what is known in endurance sports as "bonking" or "hitting the wall." This is when the body depletes all of its energy stores and starts shutting down.

Probably about an hour later my friends came rolling back down the mountain, found my lifeless body and woke me up. The remainder of the "ride" is kind of a blur, but I remember two things. The first was refusing to let them go get the car and pick me up. I *had* to finish. The second was the curious banana they fed me in an attempt to bring me back to life.

I specifically remember watching both of them pack their food into their jersey pockets before we left and it consisted of a few granola bars and a gel packet. Neither of them brought a banana; I was sure of it. Yet, somehow, they were handing me peculiarly mushy pieces of banana which I was thoughtlessly devouring aside the road. Come to find out they both had run out of food before they realized my condition. As they weighed their options of what to do with me, one of them spotted a half-eaten banana laying in the dirt on the side of the road a few dozen yards away from me which proved to be just enough calories to get me back up and over the awful mountain.

On the drive home I swore I would never touch a bicycle again. I thought I was tough, but the pain I endured that day was beyond me. It was something I didn't even know existed and it took me to one of the darkest places I had ever been.

Both of my friends were in the process of preparing for The Death Ride, which was just two weeks away. This ride consists of five mountain passes, 130 miles, and 16,000 feet of vertical elevation gain in the middle of July. Oh, and one of the mountain passes was the one that had just tried so insistently to end my life. While anyone with a vague understanding of cycling can grasp just how outrageously difficult The Death Ride is, it was unfathomable to me now after my one experience with cycling. It was impossible. My friends jokingly invited me to give it a try with them as I sat shaking and delirious in the back seat of the car. I remember not even being able to muster up a smile at the ridiculous notion.

When I got back home and slept and ate as much as a newborn elephant for a few days, my view of that experience began to change. There was just something about that level of suffering that was appealing to me. Such a simple task of riding a bicycle up a hill, or mountain, had taught me so much about myself while taking me to my absolute limits. In a single afternoon I learned just how much pain and exertion I could tolerate before my body literally shut down. Albeit, it was not nearly as fun or exhilarating as riding a motorcycle, the challenge of cycling had me mesmerized.

On a whim, I called up both of my cycling friends and told them I wanted to do the Death Ride, now just ten days away. The decision was certainly ignorant and saying I was unprepared was the understatement of the century. I don't know what it was but the challenge that this ride presented was captivating and I couldn't let it go.

I had an ancient bike that was in terrible condition, only one ride under my belt that failed miserably, and absolutely no experience or knowledge when it came to events like this. Just finishing the ride, even if it took all day, would be one of the biggest things I had ever done in my life.

Further, the symbolism was so powerful. Accomplishing a feat like this, to me, was going to be just about impossible. It was going to be miserable. It was going to hurt more than the most painful day of my life just a few days earlier, and it would last five times as long. However, if for some reason I could pull it off, I knew there was nothing that I could not pull off. If I could climb all five of those mountains, I could climb *any* mountain.

You could say the next ten days leading up to the ride were a bit like a training montage from a Rocky movie if Rocky was very tired, hungry, and constantly covered in chain grease. I started riding every day up until three days before the event. I started out at fifty miles with relatively low amounts of climbing and made it up to ninety-mile rides with almost 7,000 vertical feet of uphill. I learned so much during this week. If I drank enough water and continued to eat, I could go pretty far. If I pedaled faster in a smaller gear, my legs wouldn't get as sore. If I oiled my chain, it didn't sound like a broken locomotive coming down the road.

I had gained a little more confidence but The Death Ride still had me terrified. When the morning of the event finally arrived, I was ten times as nervous as I was for the start of any motorcycle race and my only competitor on the day would be myself.

I chose to start in the earliest wave, rolling out at 5:00 a.m. I was going to need every second I could to get this ride finished. The first three passes were filled with nerves and went by pretty quickly.

As I moved on to the fourth, the pain started to set in and visions of my epic bonk from my first ride started to creep into my mind. The biggest mental battle of my life would soon follow.

As I went over the top of the fourth pass and began descending the other side I started to regain a little composure. This was only until my rear tire exploded at forty miles per hour on the steep and winding descent. The naked rim grabbed the pavement and detonated almost half of the spokes in the wheel. It was a miracle I didn't go down. To my dismay, the bike was no longer rideable. It seemed as though it was all over.

As I walked down the mountain, a guy on the side of the road with a bike stand and a bunch of tools yelled to me, "Hey! You need some help?!"

I wanted to say no just so my aching body didn't have to get back on my bike, but the chance of still completing this epic challenge reignited some fire within me. I walked over to him and he threw my bike on his stand. He got to work while I sat on the tailgate of his truck. I still wasn't sure if he was going to be able to fix it, but the small glimmer of hope I had of completing the ride told me he'd be successful in getting my old pink Schwinn back up and running.

Sure enough, he was. I only had a few spokes left in my rear wheel and the wobble was now so bad the tire rubbed on the frame through every rotation, but it rolled. I had forty miles left and one more mountain to climb, so I got to work.

The adrenaline from my terrifying incident on the descent of the fourth pass quickly faded as I approached the last mountain. Every fiber in my body was telling me to quit. I had already made it farther than anyone thought I would. Plus, with the bike issues I was having, everyone would understand when I rolled back down to the car without the finisher badge, right? I kept trying to reason with myself to put an end to my misery that was approaching the ten-hour mark.

Fortunately, I never gave in. The idea of succeeding at such a huge challenge when the odds were against me fueled every agonizing pedal stroke. I made it to the top of the fifth and final mountain and my entire life changed. *Limits no longer existed.* If I could pick up cycling and in two weeks complete what I thought would be the death of me, what couldn't I do?

Following the Death Ride, I continued to use road cycling to train for motorcycle racing. I really had no interest to ever race road bikes, but I had strangely become affixed to the challenge of riding bicycles uphill.

I started fixing up my dad's 1984 Pro Flex mountain bike when I was a junior in high school. I figured I could get the same great training on it that my old, pink road bike provided, while also having some fun on dirt roads and trails around our house.

For anyone unfamiliar with the Pro Flex, this is the bike with the little yellow rubber pieces, called elastomers, used as suspension. Unfortunately, the bike was so old that the elastomers were petrified. Rather than compressing when I would hit a bump, they would just clank and chatter. To add insult to injury, both shifters were broken and I was always stuck in the same gear.

I loved this bike, despite the condition it was in. I could climb all of my favorite mountains that I climbed on my road bike, head onto a dirt road and climb even more. Then, rather than cruising back home on the pavement, I would pull off the road and ride home on the trails. My favorite thing to do was to chase down any spandex-wearing mountain biker and blow by them with my beat-up old bike and street clothes in an act of defiance to the cyclist I was becoming.

I had heard that there was a local high school mountain bike race series and I was very intrigued. Unlike road biking, I enjoyed ripping through the trees and rocks on my clunky mountain bike in a similar way I enjoyed it on a motorcycle. At the time, I was riding my bike to school. When class got out, I would then ride my bike, in jeans with a backpack, across town to the race. To my surprise, I won every single one.

I didn't realize it, but I had gotten pretty strong on a bicycle. On top of that, I was fearless on the downhills. This was contrary to the discomfort I had always experienced while flying down a paved descent on my wobbly road bike. I felt as though if anything was going to hurt me, it was going to be a motorcycle. So on a mountain bike, I could pin it as hard as possible because there seemed to be no consequences.

The thing I loved the most about mountain biking was not how fun and exciting it was. Sure, it was a blast and reminded me a lot of motorcycle racing, but it really does not come close to the thrill of riding a dirt bike. *What I loved most was the direct relationship between hard work and results. The harder you trained and practiced, the faster you got. Period.* As circumstances out of my control continued to derail my motorcycle racing, I could win mountain bike races just with skill and fitness. I didn't need a fancy, expensive bike, gear, parts, etc. All I needed was time and discipline to put in the work.

Fast forward to where we left off with the motorcycle chapter of my life. As my discontentment grew one broken motorcycle part after another, it seemed as though mountain biking was my escape. After the steep learning curve that came with my first road ride, the effortless success I was now having on the mountain bike trails began to bring back some of my fire that had been put out due to my moto struggles. When I finally reached a breaking point with my motorcycle racing, it was my mountain bike that I reached for.

The January that I turned twenty I made the last minute decision to not load up the truck and head to Arizona for the first round of the WORCS series. Rather, I started riding my bicycle more and more.

The decision was still to this day one of the toughest I have ever had to make. Even though I was still whole-heartedly chasing an athletic dream very similar to what I was after on a motorcycle, switching to full time mountain bike racing somewhat felt as though I was giving up – something I was taught to never do. I had dedicated my entire youth to becoming a top motorcycle racer, and now I was going to stop and pursue the same goal atop a bicycle?

On top of that, I really had no experience or promise in mountain bike racing. Sure, I could win any local junior event pretty easily, but I had no idea where I stacked up against *real* mountain bike racers. I really had no idea how to become a *real* mountain bike racer. What I needed was a coach and mentor.

I remember being at one of the local mountain bike races shortly after my big decision to take a hiatus from moto and giving the Expert category a try. I got smoked.

After the race, everyone was talking about the guy who had won. They were saying how he usually didn't race local events and gossiping about his long list of accomplishments on the bike. Turns out, that rider was Multi-Time National Champion, Kyle Dixon.

I didn't know Kyle at the time, but from what I was hearing about him, he was the best in the area and that fascinated me. I remember inviting him to ride time and time again until he was finally free one evening and we got together for a ride. He could drop me on the uphills without even breathing, it seemed.

I got to know Kyle pretty well after that and he started helping me out more and more with my riding. The day he started really training me, he asked what my goals were within the sport. He provided a few examples ranging from winning local events, all the way up to becoming a professional. Without even thinking, I told him

I wanted to race professionally and he replied with "okay" and sent me my first training plan.

Six months later, I was winning most Category 1 or Expert Men's races all over Nevada and California. This is the highest amateur classification in cycling; the next step up is Pro. I raced my first National Championships when I was twenty years old and found myself on the podium in both of my races. Immediately following Nationals, I received my pro license in the mail and was well on my way to reaching my dream.

What I had spent my entire youth trying to achieve in moto, I had done in essentially a single year on a bicycle. There was just something about the sport of mountain bike racing that clicked with me and came so much easier than in motorcycle racing. Even my mentality on a mountain bike is so much different than it ever was on a motorcycle. I was, and am still, never nervous or intimidated on a starting line. I never feel like a goal is out of reach. I feel as though I can do anything on a mountain bike, which is a feeling I've always lacked while on a motorcycle.

However, turning pro is just the first step. The real journey would begin the moment I received my professional license and it's this journey that has led me down the path that I'm on today.

There's More Than Money - Trevor

If you ask any young kid what they want to be when they grow up, I can guarantee you their answer will not be "an entrepreneur." Rather, like I've said already, you will hear things like baseball player, astronaut, pilot, chef, fashion designer, etc. But when these kids grow up? Then you will hear things like senior director of sales at some company that makes rain gutters, meat department coordinator, investment analysis advisor, etc.

As we grow up, we begin to look more at what will make us money, rather than what will make us happy. While money is obviously important, I've always felt like we shouldn't have to sacrifice happiness for it. This, to me, is entrepreneurship.

I've heard entrepreneurs are people who will do *anything* to avoid getting a job. I've also heard they are people who will do *anything* to make a buck. These are both fairly true in regards to a lot of people who will claim to be entrepreneurs.

I feel differently about entrepreneurship. To me, entrepreneurship is crafting your passion into a career. Entrepreneurship is building a successful and profitable model around the things that make you happy in life. Entrepreneurship is stepping outside of the box that society has created for all of us and finding a new and unique way of doing, creating, and progressing.

When I was six years old, a family friend was diagnosed with lupus. While my sister and I surely did not completely grasp the situation at the time, we knew there was no cure. When we inquired why there was no cure, we were told that they just hadn't found it yet.

Well, how could we help them find it? How can we speed this whole thing up so that our friend can be healthy again? These young and naïve questions led to my first "venture" you could say. My sister and I began painting rocks to look like ladybugs, selling them, and donating all of the profits to the Lupus Research Foundation.

Ridiculous, right? How is that *ever* going to help the people suffering from this terrible disease? Two children painting rocks to look like insects and then selling them to combat a disease that affects people all across the world?

It was certainly a stretch and to be honest, I don't even know if it helped, though I like to think that it did. As long as the money we donated progressed the understanding of the disease even in the slightest bit, it was a success. And just how much did we raise and donate? 30,000 dollars. A couple of kids, a lot of rocks, some paint and a few googly eyes raised and donated what, to some, is an entire year's salary. *This* is entrepreneurship.

As I got older and my racing ambitions grew stronger, entrepreneurship took a robust role in my life. I quickly learned that mall jobs and roofing houses were not conducive to my athletic goals. They took too much time and just simply did not pay enough. Not to mention, I was less than thrilled every second spent doing them.

The first business I started was at the youthful age of sixteen. It began with a talk I had with my uncle who owns an automotive repair business in the small town of Truckee, California, only about thirty miles away from Reno. He was constantly rambling about the terrible delivery services between Reno and Truckee that he was forced to deal with on a daily basis because he just had no other way of receiving the parts he needed in a timely manner. All of the services were slow, unreliable, and unbelievably expensive.

This situation, combined with my old, used, DirectTV cargo van I had purchased to haul my bikes and gear around gave me an idea. *What would it take to start my own delivery service?* Surely it would be no multi-truck operation, but I thought I might be able to pull off something that was good enough to surpass the competitors while also allowing me to work around my own schedule and make more than minimum wage.

Rather than doing the appropriate amount of research and planning, I just went for it. I created a rough business plan, some business literature explaining what I was planning to do and how to get ahold of me, and then went around to small businesses in Truckee and pitched the idea. While I think most were just excited about my young, entrepreneurial spirit, I could see some were truly interested in the business. I had competitive fees as well as a very open and flexible delivery schedule that I had come up with.

Just like that, I was off. I made a few runs between Reno and Truckee per week based upon the needs of my new clients and things began to grow quickly. The total time per run was usually about two hours, which would have translated to about $14 at the shoe store I had just quit. With my new gig? Each run would pay between $100-$500. Business was booming.

My success with the delivery service really opened my eyes to the possibilities of what can be built and created by anyone. *You really can do anything in this world, as long as you are brave enough to try it.*

As things continued to grow with the delivery business, my true passions in life began to take over a bit. In all of my fitness research, I had really started to fall in love with nutrition. The topic absolutely fascinated me and I wondered why our society doesn't put a bigger emphasis on such a paramount topic that affects the lives of everyone.

The more I learned about nutrition, the less thrilled I was about consuming different "energy bars" or athletic nutrition products. I was beginning to realize that the vast majority of the sports nutrition industry was completely ruled by clever marketing, *not* by scientific evidence. This is when the "big picture" began to form in my mind; the grand purpose to which I wanted to dedicate my life and career to.

I wanted to lead by example and combat the chronic disease epidemics that are sweeping across the country due to poor diet and lack of exercise. Further, I wanted to change the sports nutrition game by creating real-food products based upon science and research, rather than clever marketing and cheap ingredients. The plan was, and still is, to build a name for myself as an athlete by reaching the pinnacle of my sport and then use this platform to *prove* to the world the benefits of real, whole food as well as an active lifestyle. Rather than taking the route of so many other sports nutrition and health advocacy brands and just paying a top athlete a ton of money to spread my message, I want to actually show and engage the world on my own.

This idea began to completely engulf all aspects of my life. Before I turned eighteen, I made the decision to part ways with my delivery service so that I could spend my time focusing on my new nutrition business that didn't yet exist. This new venture was taking up so much of my time, it just wasn't feasible to maintain my delivery service, especially with my training and school schedules.

While I had done pretty well for myself with the delivery service and the severance, it was still a huge gamble leaving such a safe and profitable gig in order to chase a much more complex and wild idea fueled entirely by passion. But as you'll remember, passion is one of the biggest components to what makes a real entrepreneur in my opinion.

I decided to call the new enterprise GetReal Nutrition. With the help of a few partners I owned the new business with, our first sports nutrition product was a grain-free endurance energy bar. Through my own athletic endeavors I had figured out that I had a gluten allergy that was severely getting in the way of my training. As I learned more about the allergy and what causes it, I became pretty disgusted with the recipes of most of the popular bars that were available.

With no real cooking experience, I took to my parents' kitchen and began experimenting. I had a rough idea of the nutritional components I was searching for as well as the real food ingredients that would get me there. I just needed to figure out the right combination.

After several months of trial and error I came up with the perfect bar. Then came my next challenge of manufacturing, packaging, inventory, sales, etc. The logistics of running a business like this were way over my head. It was clear that I wasn't going to be able to wing it like I did with the delivery service. I needed some serious help.

I began attending networking events and meeting other successful business men and women every chance I got. It was GetReal that took my knowledge and skills to the next level and really challenged me in a different way than athletics did.

After high school, I was inspired to study dietetics at the University of Nevada, Reno. I also worked closely with several of the MBA professors on the new Entrepreneurship Emphasis that they were working on bringing to the school. All the while, I continued to build, grow, and develop this grand idea of GetReal Nutrition.

GetReal continues to be one of my primary focuses today. Over the years, I have been able to get a pretty good online setup going with manufacturing and distribution for our products. While the profits remain humble, in 2012, we were able to make our first real push towards the advocacy part of the organization. This push came in the form of my hometown's first and only youth cycling program.

While a big part of the youth program was to promote clean eating and an active lifestyle to kids in the community, I did have other motives as well. Deep down, I simply saw the need for this type of program in the Reno-Tahoe area. Despite having some of the best riding in the world, our community had barely any young cyclists. I wanted to get kids excited about something and show them the wonders of a life spent outdoors.

For me, the support and guidance I received from people like Kyle Dixon were the reason I fell so in love with the sport. It was this same mentorship and framework that I wanted to provide for other kids. The bicycle is a wonderful gift that provides so many valuable lessons, especially to young people.

What I funded with GetReal's early profits is now the nonprofit 501 (c) organization known as Reno Tahoe Junior Cycling Inc. We are the premiere developmental cycling program in the region. Further, we also have one of the largest youth cycling clubs on the West Coast.

One question I often get asked is how much money I make from RTJ Cycling. The answer is *none*. Could I monetize this great program? Sure. However, monetization of such a beneficial and genuine organization would only slow its growth and expansion, which ultimately means fewer kids on bikes. To me, this is another important quality of a good entrepreneur – *understanding there is more to life than money.*

During my sophomore year of college I met one of the most significant people to stumble into my life and our journey together would begin to define both of us. This person was Sierra Davies.

Sierra and I casually met at a barbecue for the University cycling team. I will let her explain later in this book how she ended up in Reno, but she had a certain knack for creating the most incredible and artistic things. Whether they were photos or handcrafted birthday cards, her simple creations always blew me away. On top of this, she had one of the most intense work ethics I had ever seen. She seemed to have such an incredible set of tools, just not a good direction to focus them in.

As she became more and more intertwined in my hectic life and plethora of projects, I started to have this idea of how she could focus her talents and put some organization to her amazing work ethic in order to turn her passion of creating into a career. The idea was to form a digital agency that did graphic design, web design and online marketing.

During college, I had taken a marketing internship at a local publishing office as well as a part time job as a graphic designer at the University (I did not have a lot of free time in college). I wound up in both of these positions due to my desire to strengthen my weak spots in my new venture that was GetReal Nutrition. When it comes to improving, learning is paramount. This goes for both athletics and entrepreneurship. I knew that marketing, branding, and design were going to be some of the most important keys to success for this new company so I needed to not only understand them, but become good at them. Every night I took my new skills home with me and began to put them to work on various GetReal projects.

Meanwhile, Sierra was always right by my side, just as fascinated and excited to learn about this new world of design and marketing as I was. I became very well versed in graphics, web, and marketing and so did Sierra. The result? The birth of our very own business, together, called Blü World Inspired.

Today this company is almost entirely owned and operated by Sierra. Aside from poking my nose in here and there to assist with small things, Blü World is Sierra's baby. Her growth and development into the young businesswoman she is today was amazing to watch and I'll let her discuss the process more in her own words.

Be Willing to Fail - Trevor

I graduated from the University of Nevada, Reno in the spring of 2014 with a B.S. in Dietetics and minor in Entrepreneurship. While all of my classmates were stressing over grad school or finding a high-paying job, I was actually relieved when the end of my undergrad career had arrived.

Throughout college, I had been working 40-80 hour weeks on all of my different projects, which included training, schoolwork, various marketing jobs, GetReal Nutrition, and RTJ Cycling. It would definitely be a safer bet for me to jump right into med school or perhaps a Registered Dietitian graduate program, but I had different plans.

I have always felt what sets me apart from others has been my willingness to fail. When it came to facing graduation and taking all of my various projects to the next level, turning them into one successful and meaningful career, I also was not afraid to fail. Instead, I formulated another fairly crazy idea that would allow me to continue chasing my dreams, as unattainable as they may seem to others.

Going back to my "big picture" that I had envisioned for myself and for GetReal Nutrition, my goal after college was to focus almost *entirely* on cycling. The first step in the grand idea inside of my mind was to become one of the best mountain bikers in the world in order to use my platform as an athlete for advocacy. A problem I've always had is taking on so much that the quality of my work begins to suffer due to how thin I stretch myself. Once I finished college, I vowed to dedicate every ounce of my professional life to becoming the best American mountain bike racer. Since this was the foundation to everything beyond racing that I wanted to do in my life, such as changing the nutrition industry in this country, I needed to do it right.

What exactly was the first step to becoming the best mountain bike racer in the United States? I wasn't entirely sure, but I did know that if I wanted to be the best, I had to race the best. Here in the United States, the premiere mountain bike race series is the Pro Cross-Country Tour (Pro XCT), which consists of seven races that span the country from Southern California all the way to Vermont. *This* is what I needed to be racing. This is where the biggest names in American mountain bike racing were and this is where I needed to be if I ever wanted to be one of them.

I still remember the morning when the idea came about, sitting in the kitchen of the big, empty "party boy" house that I shared with three other college friends. Sierra was over and we were having coffee and looking up some of the distances to the different Pro XCT events just for fun. We started talking about hypothetical scenarios of how we could actually make it to these faraway races, on our own, while still managing everything we had going on in our lives.

Then all of a sudden it hit both of us – *we could do this*. It would be, hands down, the craziest thing either of us had ever done, but it could be done.

The Pro XCT events, combined with some other huge races in close vicinity to our destinations would take us well over 15,000 miles across North America and last almost ninety days. All the while, I would have to build and maintain the best fitness of my life in order to stay competitive amongst the top racers in the world. Sierra would have to manage and run Blü World remotely out of coffee shops and public libraries; and we would both be dealing with the thousands of problems that would surely arise from three months of living on the road.

Was it even possible? Could we really pull it off? Was this whole thing way bigger than what we were ready for? I'd be lying if I said we knew the answer to any of those questions. Adventurous optimism prevailed though, and we decided to go for it. The adventure of a lifetime would follow.

Let Uncertainty be Your Catalyst - Sierra

I have built the path I am on today; it was not built for me. I am twenty-one years old, and I am living a life entirely different and than most people my age. I am not here because I always dreamt about this life. I am not here because I made plans to be. I am not here because I was overly fortunate, overly brilliant, or possessed any rare set of skills.

I am here because I am supposed to be here. I am supposed to be here in part because of the person I have always been, and in part because of the person I am striving to become. I made it here on a set of realizations about the kind of life I needed to live in order to feel like I was making the best use of being me. Most of these realizations came after I met Trevor, as I'll illustrate in further detail later on. He has been, and continues to be the inspiration behind everything I do. If it weren't for him, I might have never realized my true potential.

You hear a lot of stories about people making wonderful lives for themselves after they have suffered. Like a phoenix from the ashes, they bloom into a beautiful creature from a burning one. My story is not one of those. I would call it neither sad nor incredible, but I certainly feel inspiration can be attained from it.

I grew up in a very secure household. Both of my parents worked forty hours per week or more for the same company they had both been with since they were eighteen. Not only did they both work for the same company for most of their lives but they worked for a very large, very safe company: Xerox.

It was always strange to me when I found out that my friends' parents worked for small companies, or that they worked in town (mine commuted an hour each way to the big city of Sacramento) or that they got new jobs. I was accustomed to the streamlined, unchanging work lives of my parents and their huge international employer.

I have always and will always appreciate the work my parents put in to ensure that we had a nice life. I learned a lot about the value of a dollar thanks to my dad's saving habits and because my mom literally never indulged or bought herself anything, *ever*.

We had just enough hard-earned money and belongings to live a comfortable life in the Northern California countryside, but not so much that I was spoiled with lavish luxuries. We had just enough that all I ever had to worry about was doing what made me happy.

As a young child, I allowed my creative side to flourish. Nothing made me happier than when I put my imagination to use to create things with my own two hands. When my younger brother was born, I used construction paper and tape to make pacifier holders and colorful paper boxes for all of his things, usually decorated in an assortment of stickers and drawings.

Hand the "childhood me" a pair of brush clippers and I would turn dense thickets of oak and manzanita brush into a hollowed out cave that would serve as a platform for all of the lives I lived in my imagination. *Give me the tools, and let me build.* Nothing made me happier.

I even spent several years obsessed with drawing floor plans. The infinite ways a home could be laid out was fascinating. I would take free floor plan magazines from grocery stores and home improvement stores whenever I could. I learned what the symbols for doors and closets and half-walls were, and I fell in love with a giant pad of graph paper. This pad and the simple set of skills I had taught myself allowed me to design the custom floor plans to the dream homes of my imagination.

Creativity was the catalyst for my childhood happiness. It never mattered whether anyone else appreciated what I created, because I did. If I didn't like something that I made, that was fine. I could start over and keep creating until it was *perfect*.

If I was drawing a sketch of a horse (one of my favorite subjects), that horse was not done until the bumpy bones of its knees stood out. That horse was not done until every strand of mane was flying in the right direction according to the imaginary winds on the page. I used creativity to explore the world around me and to understand the ways I connected with it. It was a way for me to challenge myself to reach new heights, even if there was no final destination.

Into and throughout my teenage years, I used creativity to explore myself. I began creating vivid pictures of my life and the things that mattered to me when I got a hold of our family camera. I started to discover the kinds of stories I was able to tell through a photograph.

With creativity, curiosity and encouragement from those who enjoyed my photos driving me, I spent a year taking and editing at least one photo per day. I called it "Project 365." The project allowed me to discover more about myself in a year than I had in my entire young life. The 365-photograph collection showcased all of the events, emotions, people and places that came together to define who I was up until that point. The project symbolized the power of artistic expression in my life and solidified my love of using a camera to paint beautiful portraits of the world.

Creativity had always felt like a necessity to me. It was always something I had that I needed to let out. However, creativity did not feel like something I could use. Aside from the admiration some of my photos received, creativity did not feel like a particularly advantageous trait to have. I even forgot that I was capable of it for a while as I tried to give my life more direction. I needed to consider the bigger picture that was my future and simply being creative or taking photos did not feel very big-picture-esque. I wanted to be good at something I could use to my advantage. There was pressure to start "getting ahead" and surpassing my peers so that when the time came to apply to different colleges years down the road, I would stand out.

My parents didn't go to college, so we were all just guessing at what it would take to get in. We were doing exactly what all the counselors, books, and pamphlets said to do. We started planning for it when I was in middle school, so there was never really a question about if I would go. The only question was where I would go and what kinds of scholarships might take me there.

I needed to get good grades, so I always did. I took school very seriously, and getting a "B" was a perfectly good cause for bursting into tears.

I needed to volunteer, so I volunteered wherever I could. I helped wrap donated gifts at Christmas. I tutored weekly at my old elementary school. A friend and I even sold cookies and lemonade out of her driveway and donated the money to the Red Cross after Hurricane Katrina.

Still, I needed something else that was going to launch me from "average kid" into, well, better than average. I needed something to help me stand out, something I could call mine.

When I was ten, I discovered that I had a talent for distance running. I joined the school cross-country team in part because my best friend was on it, and in part because a family friend I greatly admire told me he *knew* I would be good at it. Sure enough, I was good at it, but I was no prodigy. Still, I felt like running could really take me places. This would be my thing. I could get *really* good at it if I worked hard enough.

I don't know if you can be naturally good at running, but I felt like I was. I had not been a natural in soccer and never even became good at it over the four years that I played. Unlike playing soccer, running felt right. It also didn't hurt that I started out near the top.

From then on, I defined myself as a runner. I ran six days a week all through high school, and I was proud that my letterman's jacket had four varsity patches on it – I never raced the lower categories. I was proud to be good at running and proud of the work I put into becoming better at it.

When I started applying to colleges and they ask you to tell them about yourself, or name a defining moment in your life, my answers were always about running. It was the only thing I had going for me, even though I wasn't the best. It gave me more to add to my résumé. It gave me more to add to the list of things that defined me, few as they seemed to be.

But the things I did in high school seemed only like a launching pad into the rest of my life. They would not carry over or amount to anything. I was a good runner, but only the greatest make a life from it. I enjoyed photography, but it seemed too hard to try to turn it into a profession.

These things were only temporary fixations to get me through adolescence, so I thought. I could not utilize them or transform them into a successful career now or in the future despite how wonderful that idea might have been.

Know When to Change Course - Sierra

It takes a certain amount of motivation and a dream strong enough to overlook possible failure to be able to venture off the comfortable path in life. I was born with some motivation, just enough to make me a little hungry for more than an ordinary life, but not enough to make me do anything about it. Some people are so motivated that they seem fearless, like nothing can stand in the way of them and their dreams. They will risk everything. Others have very little motivation and tolerance for risk, and their dreams quickly wash away as their life is molded into a design at which their childhood selves would cringe.

I was accustomed to the idea of entering a large company at a young age and then growing with it for the rest of my life, just as my parents had. That story was familiar to me and while it was not fulfilling, it was not discouraging either. That story offered security.

Aside from determining that I wanted to do something that made me happy, I spent little time considering career paths during my adolescence. There were certain things I knew I would never be happy doing. There were paths I deemed too mundane. Still, whatever I chose, I just wanted it to be exciting and I wanted to be good at it.

Aside from college application questionnaires, no one ever asked me what I planned to do with my life. No one suggested I do anything new or unique. No one encouraged me to take risks. I felt that I could choose from a list of available majors on a college website and be on my way. I would learn to love whatever career I pulled out of a hat that came after that major.

The one thing I did do was research what majors paid the highest salary and subsequently sounded interesting to me, based on the narrow view I had of the world. I chose chemical engineering because it sounded impressive and my grandmother had once told me that I had an engineer's mind and predicted I would grow up to be one. I was young when she said it, but it stuck with me. I promised myself I would learn to love chemistry and that I was meant to be an engineer.

The only other thing I did was research what kind of jobs a chemical engineering bachelor's degree could turn into. I decided I would develop biofuels, because, you know, the environment needs help and then maybe I would feel like I was doing something worthwhile on this planet. I would probably have to move to the Midwest where all of the corn is, but that decision was many years away. I didn't have to plan *that* far ahead. When the time came to decide whether or not I would continue to run in college, I decided not to. I had always planned on being a college athlete, especially since running was such a big part of who I was. But I backed out.

I was afraid of all the changes that were going to take place when I moved to college. Before I even got there and long before I started classes, I was already worried about how stressed school and running would make me. I was afraid I would never be able to compete at the college level and that I would only face failure. What should have been a decision made in strength and confidence was instead made in fear – a quality I let drive me all too often.

I chose the University of Nevada, Reno because it was close enough to home that I could go back on the weekends, but it was still far enough away to be a new and exciting experience. It is also one of the cheapest options if you are unfortunate enough to be born in the state of California, where I am certain all of the extra tuition money is being used to build a palace made of gold somewhere.

Moving to college and living in the dorms was just as wonderful and exciting as *Seventeen* magazine promises it to be. But as soon as I started taking my first engineering and chemistry classes, I panicked.

I was not thrilled to learn the material, go to class, or become a chemical engineer. I hated chemistry. I loathed my engineering classes. I was out of my element and I should have known that from the start.

I knew I was wasting my time trying to become interested in something I had no desire to pursue. Neither chemistry nor engineering clicked for me, and I knew they weren't going to. I felt like a failure because now I had to choose something else.

If I had been passionate about becoming a biofuel engineer, I might have been able to see the program through. But that plan was formed on all the wrong motives right from the start. I chose chemistry and biofuels because I thought I could make money at it and because I knew people were impressed by the title. Wouldn't my family have been proud to say that their daughter was a brilliant chemical engineer solving the world's fuel crisis? It was an irresponsible decision, and I knew it.

At that point, I should have realized that I needed to head towards doing something I liked. Instead, I made another irresponsible decision in the opposite direction.

I switched my major to accounting halfway through my freshman year on one fact and a few presumptions. The fact: I was good at math. Except I was good at formulaic math like calculus, and not the critical thinking kind of math that accounting actually requires. The presumptions: Accounting was math, and accountants made good money; therefore I could become "successful" as an accountant. I was not interested in accounting, but I was content with the idea that perhaps I could become good at it. Then maybe I would at least be making enough money to not care that I hated my job.

But I always knew that notion was wrong. Making money is not success. You can make all the money you want and never be truly successful, because what is a life full of money without happiness? Without purpose? It would be a few years before I realized that you could make a living at doing what makes you happy, and that was true success.

At the time, unfortunately, success seemed far out of reach. I was on my way to accepting an unfulfilling life with open arms and a drowned spirit. I wasn't sure if I would ever find enough motivation to do something worthwhile.

I did not want to dream up any more big dreams unless I thought that I could not fail at them. Fearing failure so deeply, I could not see that better things lay beyond the risks for those who at least tried.

I have never been good at stepping out of my comfort zone. Eventually, this would prove to be the only way for me to set forth on the right path where success is measured by happiness and purpose rather than lack of failure.

I was being pulled apart by two opposite factors – one that was concerned with having security and predictability in my life. The other was that I knew I had an untapped drive to succeed in ways that the path I was on could never reach. A very sincere part of me has always been certain that what society expected from me was undermining my potential. I wouldn't settle for average, and I would never be happy doing something that I didn't truly love. My life had so much potential that I was willing to tap into; I just lacked the courage and understanding to do so.

I knew it was possible to live a truly fulfilling life by dedicating everything to what you are passionate about. Could I ever be fearless enough, determined enough, or motivated enough to chase my passion if I learned what it was? Or would I just quit at the first signs of hardship? There had to be something out there that I was willing to commit my life to succeeding at. There had to be something that drove me enough to hang on to it at all costs. I just hadn't spent time looking for it.

Like many of my peers, I was just moving through the motions of college life. Choose a major; like it or pretend to like it; stick to it; grind through it. One of these days, something was bound to hit each of us and we would suddenly realize what our true callings were and begin to chase them. Or at least this is what we were all waiting for.

Most people don't know what they are passionate about in college, which is typically regarded as acceptable. The only problem with that is that most people get stuck there, waiting for something to take hold of their lives. For many, the waiting never stops.

Never Stop Learning - Sierra

It was around the same time that I helplessly switched my major to accounting that I also met Trevor who would inadvertently help me learn more about myself than I had ever known. I immediately realized that Trevor possessed qualities that I had never seen at work in another human being. He had huge dreams, and he had already gone great lengths to turn them into reality. He was working vigorously towards accomplishing the things that would make his life successful. That is, success measured by happiness and prosperity, not just money.

He was turning his dreams into reality. Clearly, he would never be the kind of person to settle for an ordinary life. He was already a thousand paces in front of me, heading in the direction I wanted to be going.

I began to tag along down the path he was on – the one I yearned to be on but felt I didn't yet deserve. I wanted to find a way to prove to him that I was worth his precious time. I could chase my dreams like that too, if I could just figure out what they were.

Trevor had found a way to put his motivation to use while I was still waiting for something to strike a fire within me. I needed to be injected with motivation to accomplish even a fraction of what he was doing. *He was creating a truly extraordinary life, one risky, yet calculated, step at a time.*

For months, I took in Trevor's life and tried to understand the things he did and the choices he made. He had no problem spending every last minute of his spare time working, responding to emails, arranging deals, and meeting people. He would rather stay in and talk to me about the ideas he had than go out and spend time at parties or with friends. He was always busy in a way that I had yet to understand. There was always something that needed to be done.

At the time, I worked at The Home Depot. All *I* had to worry about when I got home was how to get the paint stains I had acquired at work out of my pants. The more I understood and adapted to the life that Trevor lived, full of unending ideas and things to do, the more he allowed me to help him. One of the first things I began to learn was graphic design. Trevor's personal and business ventures alike always required designs for various things – cycling gear and t-shirts, Facebook cover photos and Twitter background images, business cards, fancy images for all of his current websites, etc.

On top of everything else he was working on, Trevor had just taken a new marketing job at a local publishing company. Everything he was involved in required marketing of some sort, *so it was more effective to learn these skills than pay someone else.* Since I was starting to help with all of his ventures, it only made sense that I learn these skills too, but I was nowhere near qualified enough to get a job like that. Instead, Trevor got me the software he was using at the new job, and then he would come back and teach me skills he was acquiring. He would teach me the basics, at least, and then it was up to me to figure out the rest.

Having a background in photography, I took what Photoshop skills I had and I transferred them to Illustrator, the industry standard graphic design program. I spent countless frustrating hours trying to make the creations in my imagination appear on the computer screen. Five-year-olds could have made better art with a piece of paper and some crayons.

Immediately, I wanted to give up. I was embarrassed at how bad I was at designing with Illustrator. Plus, I didn't want to disappoint Trevor when he trusted me with these projects. However, I figured he would probably be more disappointed with no design than with a bad one. Instead of giving up, I began to soak in what I could. I learned from Trevor when he was available to teach. I attempted tutorial books and discs. I read books about design. We even sat through an eight-hour online class together and then I watched countless other online tutorials to make my designs come to life. I continued practicing. I *loved* the idea of design and I *wanted* to become good at it.

If I thought learning Illustrator in a few week's time was an accomplishment, it is now a mere strand in the web of learning that followed. As Trevor continued to trust me with all of his growing projects, I continued to need to learn more. Trevor taught me what he could in the spare time he had each day, which was very little. The rest of the time, I struggled, stressed, and fretted over teaching myself things I knew nothing about. I got frustrated, I got angry, and I wanted to quit often. I got so hung up on the end goal and still feared failure greatly. I really didn't want to fail Trevor, of all people.

When it came to designing things, I took my work very seriously and very personally. To me, being creative had always been about making things for myself. It never mattered what other people thought, so I could never really fail at it. When I started using my creativity to design things for Trevor and the people he worked with, I was often faced with criticism that I didn't know how to accept. Of course, this is how graphic design works, because it is hard for one person to create something out of someone else's imagination. Not realizing that, I took these instances personally, and it took me a long time to accept that I was not *failing*. I was *learning*.

Understand What Drives You - Sierra

After months of helping Trevor with his own business ventures and various other projects, he proposed the idea that we start a business together using all the skills he had and the ones I was learning. I thought I knew what it meant to own a business because Trevor had a few, and I saw the excruciatingly hard work it took to make those businesses successful. Seeing it from the outside is one thing, but experiencing it from within is a different beast entirely.

I had no idea what it would mean to go into business for myself – to dedicate one hundred percent of my time and energy to working for something I actually cared about – to become an *entrepreneur*.

When Trevor proposed the idea, I had just left my very fun but not exactly fulfilling job at The Home Depot in favor of a much less fun job as a database manager for a local branch of a large real estate company. I made the switch only because I knew I had to have more on my résumé than "professional paint mixer." I thought the new job might give me a better sense of purpose because it required a little more brainpower than mixing paint – *It didn't*. I worked endless hours pressing the "copy" and "paste" buttons on a computer and sealing envelopes. If nothing else, I became very good at high-speed envelope stuffing.

I couldn't wait to leave that dull job but I was also afraid of moving my life forward. That office job was secure. I could have any time on or off I wanted. I was guaranteed ten dollars for every hour I sat in my chair, whether or not anything came of it. Starting and then running a business would change all of that. It did not occur to me that becoming an entrepreneur could be the first step

I had to take to create a fulfilling, successful life for myself. I did not immediately see how it would allow me to obtain the happiness and freedom in my career I had always wanted but never knew how to find. At first, it just sounded very difficult and scary.

Luckily, I didn't even have a chance to back out of this opportunity. I don't think it mattered how I felt about the venture, because Trevor was already pushing us forward. The idea quickly took hold and our own design and marketing company was on its way to becoming reality. There was so much to learn before the business could become licensed and official. I had been oblivious to the work it would take. A lot of personal changes in myself would also have to take place before I could run a business.

I was used to being told what to do in a work environment. I lacked initiative and organizational skills. I stressed and broke easily. I needed to be able to ask questions. Now I couldn't ask questions because I was teaching myself how to do *everything* our new business plan said we could do.

Trevor seemed to know how to do it all, and he taught me just enough that I started blowing gaskets trying to figure the rest out. I quickly learned that he was in no mood to sit around and answer all of my questions, especially when he knew that if I just tried harder and dug deeper, I could answer most of them on my own.

I was almost always frustrated and on the edge of breaking down for the first few months. I had never been more stressed in my life. Why did Trevor think I was capable of running this business with him when I knew only a fraction of what I needed to know? When I still wasn't very good at the few things I *had* learned?

We had wanted to start the business with more people than just the two of us, because more people meant we would eventually be able to take on more clients. More people should mean more skills on the table. Unfortunately, I learned more people did not actually mean more work was getting done.

As I continued to spend all of my spare time working, learning and pushing the business towards inception, the others did not. There was a lot to be done, and there were a lot of instances where it was easier to step away than push through. All those who had eagerly jumped on board just as eagerly jumped off when serious work needed to be done. Not that long ago, I might have done the same. Now, I was working towards something I was actually excited about.

Still, for every ounce of excitement I contained, there was another ten ounces of pressure. I wasn't sure how long I would last until I eventually cracked and crumbled beneath it. I could not continue to live under such constant stress for long. It felt like I was failing at every project I undertook. *Start. Start over. Fine tune. Finish. Deliver. Get feedback. Scrap it. Start over. Again and again.* I spent so much time re-doing things, there was nothing else I could think to call it but *failing.*

Finally paying the hundreds of our own hard-earned and scarce dollars, and filling out the piles of paperwork to make Blü World Inspired a real, legal business was frightening and wonderful. A business now existed that could *only* exist as long as I continued to pump life into it. There was absolutely no quitting at this point. I owned a business and I still didn't know if I wanted to own a business.

As scary as it felt, I decided I did want to own this business. After all of the hard work I had put in for the last year, something had finally clicked in me. I *did* have enough drive to be successful at this; at being an entrepreneur.

Take Calculated Risks - Sierra

Being in business was something I could finally be proud of. Even though sometimes I felt like I was failing, I knew the business would only *truly* fail if I gave up. It was safe to say that I was never going to become an accountant. I am still in school to earn my degree and to use the knowledge I gain to keep the financial aspects of life and business in check. However, I no longer feel the need to settle somewhere just because it provides security. Instead, I am willing to take the necessary risks and pay the necessary costs to create a life of passion, purpose, and freedom.

The work continued to pile on as our names spread through the local business community. It finally came time for me to leave my database job at the real estate company. While I *was* relieved to leave that place that offered no sense of fulfillment, it also meant officially leaving a path that was safe and common. Instead, I would be stepping with both feet onto a path that still needed building. Plenty of unknowns were lying ahead.

Leaving that job meant leaving behind the old Sierra. It meant leaving behind that person who was going to settle for something she didn't love. I was happy to leave those parts of her behind and take only the parts that longed to dream big and build a life fueled by passion. I was now an entrepreneur with endless open doors waiting for me to walk through. It was new, invigorating, and terrifying.

Aside from all of the work that had to be done on a daily, no, *hourly* basis, I now had even more to worry about. Getting a paycheck every other week was no longer a certainty. If I did not meet all my deadlines and perform well, the business was coming down with me. I wasn't sure how to allocate my time, especially when there never seemed to be enough of it. How much longer was it acceptable to study before I needed to get the rest of my work done for the night? Or, if I tried to get all my work done first, what if there was no time left to study? Even that was a silly question because the work never was and never *is* done. There was always more fine-tuning, organizing, planning and more learning to be had.

Everything was changing faster than I could keep up with. With this new life whirling all around me, I was too busy to even notice the changes happening within myself. When new projects came in, *I stopped being afraid of failing at them and started becoming excited at the opportunity to succeed. I finally stopped doubting myself in everything I did.*

Most of all, I was proud of myself for all of the hard work I had put in to build this business despite all of the costs. Everything that Blü World Inspired was becoming was a product of the work that Trevor and I put into it. We were entirely and solely responsible for creating something impressive and beautiful. No one else could claim it.

As a child, I spent my happiest days making things and using my imagination. Now, my passion for creation is fueling my job. On my own, I get to make something of myself that is bigger and brighter than anyone ever expected, myself included. Becoming the owner of a business I am passionate about was only the beginning of the changes that my life was experiencing. Every situation I approached was framed by the hard work I had been putting in day after day for quite some time.

Things that used to seem huge were no longer large feats. Cranking out a ten-page economics paper was no worse than writing a ten-page business proposal for a new client. As long as I made my mind up to get something done, work or school, I could sit down and work and work and work until it was a masterpiece.

As I learned to allow stress to motivate me rather than paralyze me, I became more productive. Suddenly I could accomplish so much more in an hour. Driving twenty minutes from campus to personally deliver a large order of business cards and then driving back before my next class in a forty-five minute gap was cutting it close, but there was no time to waste.

I used to be the kind of person that, if I had to work at The Home Depot from ten in the morning until seven at night, I considered my day entirely exhausted. Now, I would grab the old me by the shoulders, shake her, and tell her she is crazy to not see how many hours there are before ten and after seven. The old Sierra could have been putting those hours to use, but she never did. She never had anything to chase after. She never had the amount of motivation that entrepreneurship created for me. Now, I was entirely in control of my present and my future.

Plan for Expansion - Sierra

It didn't take terribly long for me to realize what Trevor had known all along. Starting a business was only the beginning. We were capable of so much more and had no reason to stop here. We were young. We were making a living for ourselves, by ourselves. We could go anywhere and do anything we have passion for. We just had to decide what to tackle next.

Trevor was graduating from the University of Nevada, so all of a sudden it felt like it was time to do something big. I still had one year left, so technically I was approaching my last summer break, which would prove to be no "break" at all.

Trevor's biggest vision involved becoming the top American mountain biker. He wasn't going to get there unless he could race with the top riders in the country. He couldn't race with the top mountain bikers without traveling to the largest races across the continent. We had to find a way to get there.

Could we even do it? To race the right races, we were going to have to drive to all of them, and since they were all so far away from home, we would need to be on the road for nearly three months straight. We would need some kind of vehicle to live in. No one was footing the bill for us and we needed help offsetting the cost of gas, race entry fees, hotels, and all the other expenditures that we would incur along the way.

It sounded crazy, and that part of me that likes to doubt myself so much was not sure if we could really pull all of those strings together. But wasn't "crazy" exactly what we lived for? Were we not extremely adept at pulling together what no one else could?

If Trevor wanted to make this dream happen, and if I wanted to go with him, then we would. We were not accustomed to letting anything stand in our way.

Nothing extraordinary ever gets done in this world unless there are people willing to dream dreams that everyone else thinks are too big. The first step was planting the idea in our own minds. It was sitting right in front of us, a tiny seed, asking if we were going to water it, give it soil and sunlight.

That morning in the kitchen of Trevor's house, we considered each other with widened eyes, reading each other's faces and wondering if the other was serious. The trip was how many miles? 15,000, minimum. We would have to drive for how many weeks? Around eleven, maybe more. We would sleep where? Well, we would have to buy a van or something to travel and live in.

The idea itself was straight out of a classic summertime movie, with all the right ingredients and flare. Well, at least it seemed that way for now. Years ago, I would have jokingly dreamt about such an adventure with friends late at night. Don't we all want to set down the heavier parts of our lives and take off on a paper-thin dream? *But, what if we could?*

Part 1 – Planning for the Unknown

Believe in Yourself - Trevor

I've always felt like waiting until you are "ready" is often the biggest mistake people with incredible talents and potential make. Sure, some times are better than others to make huge leaps of faith, but in the end, that's what it comes down to – faith. Belief in yourself and in your dreams, no matter how crazy they seem to others, is key to doing anything extraordinary in this world.

When it came to this three-month race tour of North America's largest mountain bike events that Sierra and I decided to pursue, we were far from ready. In fact, you could even make a strong argument that the timing was terrible for such an endeavor; two twenty-some-thing-year-olds tied down by school and a variety of other hopeful projects with a college-student budget. Was this really the time for touring North America and pursuing such incredible goals?

As I continued to battle my own doubt and worries about the risks associated with the journey, Sierra and I set a departure date of June 5th. This would give us about five months to plan and prepare for the biggest challenge of our young lives, while still managing and developing all of the various projects we had going on.

There have been several times in my life where I have bitten off more than I could chew. This has always been a knack of mine. I think this is partly because I don't always think things through, but I also just love getting myself into situations that force me to push my limits, or fail. Surely, planning for this journey was going to either push me to new heights or provide one of the most epic failures of my life.

The first thing I needed to tackle was the exact race schedule and travel itinerary. I decided the first stop would be GoPro Mountain Games in Vail, Colorado. Next, we'd continue through the Rockies and spend some time in Colorado Springs with two friends of ours who were now living there. Then we'd head north to Missoula, Montana for a Pro XCT. After that we would loop back down to Colorado Springs for another Pro XCT, while making a bit of a side trip to hit Coeur d'Alene and Boise, Idaho for yet another project I was working on that we will discuss more later.

Next, we would begin to head east with our first stop being Lawrence, Kansas. We would then visit Racine and Madison, Wisconsin, before hitting another Pro XCT in Portage, Wisconsin. From here, the racing would really begin to pick up as we headed even further east. After a quick stop in Muncie, Indiana we would be off to Macungie, Pennsylvania for USA Cycling Mountain Bike National Championships and then up to Williston, Vermont for the final Pro XCT of the season.

As long as my body and bikes were still in one piece at this point, we would then cross the border into Canada for the World Cup in Quebec before dropping back down into America for the last North American World Cup in Windham, New York. After this, the only thing left to do would be to make the fifty-hour drive back home to Nevada.

In a sport where it often takes a decade for athletes to reach their potential, I was only entering into my third year as a mountain bike racer and just my second year as a professional. While I was having a ton of local and regional success, I was virtually unknown on a national level.

I was fortunate enough to land a pretty solid sponsorship program locally from Audi and the bicycle manufacturer Specialized at the start of 2014. While I wasn't taking home a paycheck, Audi and Specialized provided me with two of the best mountain bikes on the market, all of the gear I needed, and a network of extremely supportive individuals that I had never had in the cycling world before.

However, when it came to the traveling and various expenses and challenges that come with the 15,000-mile adventure we were planning, we were entirely on our own. While my competitors would all be flying to the events, airfare was certainly not in our budget. This created our first big challenge, which was finding a vehicle.

When I made the switch to full-time mountain bike racing, I sold my cargo van and got a small, fuel-efficient car instead. After only one season of driving to races in my little two-door hatchback with no air conditioning, I was over it. The car was so small, we actually had to unbolt the rear row of seats and remove them in order to fit my bikes inside. On top of that, I had to take both the front and rear wheels off of my bikes every time I loaded them up into my little go-cart of a vehicle in order for them to fit. It just wasn't practical and surely would not suffice in transporting bikes, gear, and belongings all across the continent. So I sold it and began the search for a more suitable travel vehicle.

We decided on getting another cargo van because aside from being able to fit bikes and belongings inside of it, we could also sleep in it, thus eliminating lodging expenses. Who needs to pay fifty dollars for a cheap motel when you have a van and a Wal-Mart parking lot, right?

I set a budget for the new race rig at $8,000 and we had about four months to find it. For anyone who has ever been in the market for a used van, you can understand just what type of vehicles you find around this price point. For weeks, I scoured the Internet without seeing a single van that I thought would even make it to the Utah border, let alone all the way to Quebec. For the first time, significant doubt started to creep into my mind and made me question if the whole endeavor was really attainable. We hadn't even left yet and the challenges already seemed insurmountable. If we couldn't even find a vehicle, how could we plan on road tripping across the continent for three months?

Just as quickly as the negativity had come on, it disappeared with the discovery of several worthy van candidates in Southern California. I was filled with hope again, and reminded of the resilience and positivity that were going to be necessary to be successful on this journey. Surely, this would be just one small hurdle compared to what was coming.

Between school, training, and work I made the trip down to Southern California to check out vans. I drove down with my dad, who was still 100 percent behind my racing passion despite my decision to trade in a motor for pedals. It was the first long drive we had been on in years since I hung up the moto boots, as I typically made the journey to mountain bike races on my own.

The first vehicle I wanted to see was a 2004 Ford Econoline passenger van. It had a small V8 motor in it with tinted windows all around the silver body. While it had a few dents and scratches, it was in incredible shape. With only 58,000 miles on it and an asking price of $8,900, this was hands down the best van I had seen in my price range throughout my weeks of hunting.

The owner was a pretty unique gentleman who lived in Venice Beach, California. Aside from his numerous stories regarding close encounters with Lindsay Lohan, whom he claimed lived just down the street from him, he was absolutely convinced throughout our entire interaction that I was conning him somehow. The story of a twenty-two-year-old from Reno driving nine hours through the night *just* to look at his family van didn't add up.

As he continued to question my motives, I began to fall in love with Ol' Silver. Sure, she was already ten years old, but she had character. Like fine wine, this van had only gotten better with age. Well, that's what I was telling myself since this was quite literally the *only* van I could afford that seemed decent.

After taking the van for a test drive, I spent almost two hours inspecting every inch. I knew this purchase was going to set the tone for our entire trip and I only had one shot at it. There were a few things that I stumbled upon that I was wary of. One of them was a weird weld on the hinges of the side doors, making it seem as though they had been re-attached for some reason. On top of this, they seemed to not shut correctly. Another issue was some strange wires hanging out of the backup camera that he had installed into the dash. It was as if he had gotten frustrated or confused during the installation process and just quit. But hey, it still kind of worked.

While he had relatively understandable explanations for both things, something didn't sit well with me. The motor, chassis, and transmission were my biggest focuses and they were all in great shape, but these small cosmetic issues seemed as though they might be a big problem down the road. I just wasn't sure exactly how…

Still, this van was in a league of its own compared to every other one I had found. Even the other options I had set up to go look at next that day down in Southern California had almost twice as many miles and were well over $9,000. When the owner agreed on a very low final price of $7,800, I took the deal. As hard as I tried, I couldn't find a reason *not* to get this van, and I was confident I would easily be able to resell it when we got back home in the fall for no less than what I had paid for it.

Just twenty-six hours after departing for L.A. I arrived back home with a shiny, new (to me at least) van that would soon be our home and mobile office. We began prepping the inside of Ol' Silver for her maiden voyage. The first order of business was removing the center row of seats. The newly created space would serve as our kitchen, office, garage, bedroom, and lounge.

Next, I paid my dad a visit and we crafted a four-bike platform stand in the back. This consisted of a piece of plywood that sat about a foot off of the floor of the van. On the top of it were four mounts that attached to the front forks of mountain bikes. We now had a spot for both of my beautiful new Specialized race bikes, my practice bike, and Sierra's bike. Underneath the platform served as extra storage. However, it was becoming apparent that we were going to need a lot more space than what was available inside of the van. Fortunately, we stumbled upon a solution for that purely by chance.

My uncle from Truckee had recently received a totaled Subaru at his automotive repair shop that the owner had ditched. Atop the sad wagon was an enormous Thule "roof rocket" storage box. It was absolutely ancient and in terrible condition. Filled with dirt and leaves, the outer coat of paint was almost entirely pealed off and the lock and hinges were covered in rust and corrosion.

When I first saw it, I was less than hopeful. But given the circumstances, I started cleaning it up to see if there was any way it could work. To my surprise, the box was mechanically pretty sound. While it looked awful, it was functional, which was the only thing that mattered. Now, all we needed was a roof rack to put on the van to mount it to.

This takes us to our next fortunate secondhand acquisition in the form of an old, bulky roof rack. My dad just so happened to have this lying around behind his house from an old work van he had almost a decade prior. Sure enough, it fit my van like a glove. Our new roof storage setup was quite the sight, but it got the job done. Just like my clunky first bicycle, I didn't need anything fancy, I just needed *something* and I was unbelievably grateful to have it. *This is what an entrepreneur would refer to as "bootstrapping."*

Bootstrapping is doing the most with the very least. It is thinking outside of the box in order to accomplish something with severely limited resources. Or, in other words, bootstrapping is the ability to not let your limited resources dictate your future.

My entire life has been bootstrapped. Everything from my finances to my time has become very limited. Because of this, I try to invest in creative and unique ways to reach my goals, while sometimes sacrificing things like aesthetics. My lifestyle is far from lavish because of this, but it is also going in a direction that I think most people in my position would view as impossible.

The money we saved by running this obnoxious but free roof setup could now be used to purchase ten more tanks of gas and get us an additional 4,000 miles across North America. I wasn't going for style points, I was going for race results; and the only way I could get those was if I made it to the races.

With the new (old) van set up and ready for action, the next big hurdle was figuring out the finances behind such a feat. Between sponsorships, Blü World, and our various other projects, we would need to be able to feed ourselves, fill up the van, pay for entry fees, and be prepared for any surprises that may arise during the three months of travel. While money surely isn't everything in life, it is a necessary variable that absolutely can't be ignored.

This is something I often find can be misinterpreted when it comes to both ambitious, as well as passionate people. Those who are ambitious tend to be labeled as also being infatuated with money. Those who are extremely passionate and spend their life pursuing their dreams tend to be labeled as broke and uninterested in contributing to society. For me, I like to think that a healthy balance of both is what creates true success. Sure, spending the rest of my life traveling the world and racing my bike would be wonderful. However, if it means that once I retire I have to open up a taco stand just to make enough money to put gas in my van that still doubles as my home, well, that doesn't seem like success to me.

If I do nothing more than race bikes, what is my contribution to society? What is my impact on the world? I may be a little young for getting this philosophical, but I want to leave this planet a better place than it was when I got here. I want my work to mean something. Passion with a proper plan behind it can do just that.

For me, racing is simply the platform atop of which I want to build my legacy. It just so happens to also be my passion and one of the things I love most in this world. By using every ounce of my ambition to achieve excellence on my bike, I hope to craft a lucrative career that will allow me to have financial freedom later in life. At the same time, I can build a platform to inspire, educate and motivate others to chase *their* dreams and find this balance that I believe to be paramount to true success in life.

During my final weeks of college before graduation, I took a part-time job at a local cycling startup company called TrainerRoad as a "Marketing Specialist." TrainerRoad is a software company that allows cyclists to train at home on stationary bike trainers while receiving live, biometric feedback via the TrainerRoad application on their computer. With this technology, you can do structured workouts based upon power or heart rate from the comfort of your own home.

I met the brilliant minds behind this awesome company in 2013 after I had been invited to ride on Team USA at the World Cup in Quebec. We were connected via our local entrepreneurship community, and they helped offset some of the costs of this incredible racing opportunity that I had just one year prior.

They knew I had several projects I was working on and they admired my desire to learn and improve as an entrepreneur and cyclist. As TrainerRoad began to completely take off, they offered me a job at the rapidly expanding company; providing me just another opportunity to learn and hone in my skills as an entrepreneur in a cycling-focused environment. It was an honor. I had so much on my plate at the time and was in no way looking for work. However, the chance to work on the ground floor of such a young, promising cycling and fitness company was one I could not turn down. I was absolutely thrilled by the offer and adjusted my hectic schedule to make it work.

The only thing I was concerned about was the race tour I had planned. Before accepting the job, I told the owners about it and they were surprisingly excited. As long as I could find Wi-Fi along the way, they were more than happy to let me work on the road. They were especially excited because it just so happened my scattered race schedule fit together perfectly with an enormous project they were in the early stages of.

This project required someone to obtain real video footage and GPS data from famous triathlon and cycling courses all across the continent. Once they had the GPS files and video footage, they would then create TrainerRoad workouts based upon the profile of the course. Next, they would sync up the video to the workout and users would be able to virtually ride courses all across North America from the comfort of their home. It's an absolute "game-changer" in the endurance sports world.

With the majority of the courses that they wanted to target being pretty close to our planned summer route, they asked me to help tackle the data and footage acquisition part of the project. While it was sure to add some extra stress and challenges to what was already a fairly massive endeavor, I was thrilled to be a part of such an exciting project.

TrainerRoad provided us with five GoPro cameras, five extremely long micro USB cables, five wireless remote controllers, five suction cup mounts, and tons of extra batteries and memory cards. The plan was to mount the GoPro cameras all around the outside of my van, then feed the USB cables from an inverter on my dash out the windows to all of the cameras. With some of the courses being well over one hundred miles long, this was the only way we could make the batteries inside of the cameras go the distance.

Then, we would simply drive around the courses maintaining a speed of thirty miles per hour. While we had no experience with GoPro cameras, filming, or anything remotely close to this kind of a project, it seemed simple enough. Unfortunately, we would soon learn the hard way just how difficult the task could be.

Before we left and while we were away, we would have income from TrainerRoad, Blü World Inspired, and GetReal Nutrition. However, we had to factor in a bit of a lull in Blü World work and GetReal sales since we would have less time to focus on them. This was fine, as the big picture rewards of a successful summer tour would surely make up for the temporary low profits that we were anticipating. However, this left us cutting it extremely close in terms of finances for 15,000 miles of traveling and three months of living on the road. It could be done on the budget we had, but it would be tight. As discussed earlier, my sponsorships at the time were almost entirely on a local basis. Meaning if I wanted to drive my van to Quebec and race a World Cup, I was on my own.

Since the race season had already begun, I knew it would be quite the task to obtain any new sponsorships on such short notice, especially financial ones. However, I figured that at least reaching out and meeting different people within the industry would only benefit me down the road.

Racing my bike around the world was something I wanted to continue to do. Even more, it was something I wanted to continue to do as my profession. I was fine with living in a van this year as a means to an end. Going for days without a shower and pumping up an air mattress every night before going to bed was no problem at this stage of my career. But I needed to start setting things up for the future because this lifestyle was certainly not conducive to the long and illustrious career I wanted.

With this in mind, I began reaching out to various businesses and individuals, both locally and all across the country. Through my entrepreneurial community as well as my ever-expanding cycling network, I had a solid list of people to start with.

I didn't ask a single person I talked with for money. Rather, I asked them for advice. Even though we could have used some extra cash, I understood the value of a dollar and I knew I quite frankly was not worth a huge financial endorsement at the time, especially on such short notice with such little planning.

By asking for advice and looking for conversation, I was able to talk and connect with everyone on a much deeper level than had I just been after money. My main goal was to create strong relationships that I could then utilize down the road as I began to establish myself as a top rider in the country. I needed to do this in order to earn the endorsements I needed to keep my racing career alive and well.

On top of that, these various business men and women from within the cycling industry who I talked to shared with me exactly what they looked for in their athletes. Essentially, they told me what I needed to do in order to be worthy of their money down the road. This was something I did all wrong during my motorcycle days. Sure, my jump to the top was unplanned and premature, but I had done absolutely nothing to create any kind of safety net for myself in the form of strong relationships within the industry. What should have been an amazing opportunity turned into a nightmare because I was so shallow in my pursuit.

It's true that the most important part of being a professional athlete is how well you perform. However, it's also a business. At the end of the day, athletes are paid because they help sell products. You may be incredible at what you do, but if no one knows who you are or likes you as a person, why would anyone ever pay you to compete?

When you get to the point where you begin to consider turning sport into a profitable career, who you know and how you present yourself are two very important things. I had learned this the hard way once and I wanted to make sure I didn't make that mistake again moving forward in my young mountain biking career.

One of the biggest supporters of my racing is the president of Reno-Tahoe Audi Cycling, Don Pattalock. While Audi was really only a road cycling team for master's racers (amateur racers, typically over the age of thirty), Don had gone to extra lengths to leverage the relationships he had through his organization to bring my junior cycling program and myself under his umbrella of support.

Don is also the man who connected me with Specialized. At the top level of the sport, having a strong, efficient, and light bike is extremely important, but elite mountain bikes can cost upwards of $15,000. Don completely went out on a limb for me to get two of the finest bicycles Specialized makes so I had one less thing to worry about when I line up with the worlds best riders. This gesture is one I will never forget and will always be grateful for.

When I met with him to talk about my plans for the summer, he immediately offered to put together a fundraiser for me. While I respectfully declined his offer, this just goes to show you the type of guy Don is. He wants to see me succeed just as badly as I want to see myself succeed. It was inspiring to say the least. Still, I was not looking for free money.

With a sponsorship, the athlete is responsible for helping that company generate sales. Both parties are bringing something to the table. With a fundraiser, people would just be handing me money for nothing. Had my financial circumstances been a little more grim perhaps I would have accepted his offer. However, I knew I could pull the whole thing off with my current resources. I wanted to pay my dues and suffer on my own dime before I accepted anyone else's in exchange for nothing.

However, I was fortunate enough to receive a small amount of additional financial assistance in the form of a sponsorship from two local entrepreneurs I look up to tremendously. Mike Henderson and Jim Scripps own the bicycle light company, Jet Lites. It's a Reno-Tahoe based company totally changing the night riding game with their incredible products.

While Mike and Jim are both avid mountain bikers, neither of them follow the racing scene very intently. Still, they were psyched about everything I was doing and my hunger to reach such high goals within the sport. We got together and talked several times about the tour. They just genuinely wanted to help in any way they could.

Being a young, growing business, Jet Lites was in no position to throw a huge check at me. But they did offer some financial assistance in exchange for writing blogs, distributing information and spreading the word of their brand. Then, they also began connecting me with more and more successful and powerful people who could further assist me.

I remember being at the Jet Lites grand opening party and going around with Jim as he introduced me to the various people there. Several of them asked if he was my agent, as Jim had shared so much about me with most of the people at the party even before that night. I was honored. Mike and Jim had my back so much that they were out there trying to land me new sponsors and contacts even when I wasn't with them. These were the kind of people I needed in my corner.

Something I never shared with anyone, including Sierra, was just how terrifying the whole idea of this trip was to me. On the surface, it may seem fairly simple – just driving to mountain bike races for a few months. But really, it was so much more than that.

Our entire lives would be stuffed into a metal box on wheels that I really knew nothing about aside from what the online listing said. Would it make it to Colorado? Would it make it to Wisconsin? Would it make it to Quebec? Even if it did make it to all of our destinations, would it make it *back*?

If the van didn't survive... Well, I tried to push those kinds of thoughts out of my head. I had enough money in the bank to *maybe* fix a semi-catastrophic mechanical failure. Now factor in the risk of failure that also came along with my bikes, our computers, and Sierra's photography and videography equipment and we were really walking a fine line.

As much as I hated the thought, there was a certain margin of luck that we were depending on in order to survive the trip. If something were to go seriously wrong, we had no safety net. There was no one we could call to bail us out nor was there a "plan B." If things took a turn for the worse, it would be entirely up to us to come up with a solution, no matter how impossible it may seem.

I've been fortunate enough to love so much more than to fear in life. My love for mountain bike racing, adventure, and the pursuit of my dreams will always outweigh my fear of failure. This love is what I choose to let dictate my decisions, not my fear.

Even more, I had to be strong for Sierra. As she began to dive into her own vast list of planning duties, surely the same fears would begin to overwhelm her. When they did, I wanted her to be able to seek comfort and strength from me, rather than even more doubt and worry.

Make the Most of Everything - Sierra

At first, I was rolling my eyes at the whole idea. This trip was too big and there was just too much that absolutely had to come together without incidence for it to actually work out. Half of me knew it was possible because we always managed to pull off the goals we set for ourselves. The other half of me was in a panic, thinking, "We don't have enough time to put this whole thing together."

Having the foresight to plan every detail of a weeklong vacation is tough. Planning every detail of a three-month-long adventure is tougher. Planning a road trip, ten huge bike races, three months worth of work *and* all the other facets of our lives for three months was crazy.

The amount of time that we could dedicate to planning this trip didn't even exist. It would have been nice to set aside an hour each night towards planning. Maybe an hour could be spared before bed when schoolwork and business-work were done. Unfortunately, those spare hours had vanished from my once-simple life. I hadn't known what free time was for over a year. Blü World Inspired and schoolwork consumed my every hour, and if I needed to help Trevor with GetReal or anything else, it was already a tight squeeze for time. Add trip planning to the pile and my days were over-booked.

I typically had a few choices every day that competed for my attention. Do I spend the next hour studying for my exam tomorrow? Should I write my client's blog post I needed to have done by the end of the week? Or, should I try to brainstorm ways to help Trevor in his quest for sponsors, even though we were months away from departure?

I like to cross things off the perpetually lengthening list in my mind, so it always feels better to finish the items with an earlier due date first. In my brain, it's a first-due-first-done system. This made it difficult to find time to plan the trip months in advance. There always seemed to be more pressing issues nagging in the back of my mind.

Still, no matter how hard I wished for it, the trip was not going to organize itself and the time to plan it was not going to magically appear. I had no free time, but I also had no time to wait. If I did not pull through on planning my end of the trip, then it would not matter how much Trevor got done. The reality was, if I did not deliberately make time each week, then it was not going to happen.

That's why I had to find a balance between getting the things done that needed immediate attention, and slowly chipping away at completing this immense task. I wanted to put it off because it was so overwhelming and it still seemed so far away, but I knew that the weeks had a way of flying by without much being accomplished.

My list of planning obligations was something like: make the sponsorship proposal, help to get sponsors, prepare and secure Blü World Inspired for the journey, plan and carry out marketing strategies to expose the trip to the public, and then some.

The sponsorship proposal was the first thing that I had to get done. We weren't sure what we were going to get from potential sponsors on such short notice, but we had to try. Getting money would be a stretch, but any assistance in making the trip easier or promoting it would make a huge difference. Any help we could find would expose us to more people and extend our reach.

Creating the sponsorship proposal reminded me of writing the business plan for Blü World Inspired – a task I never wanted to relive. Before anything can happen, you have to be able to predict everything that you will encounter, without leaving any details to chance. For Blü World, that meant determining our market, analyzing our competitors, and setting up our business practices before we even had a client. We just had to assume how our client relationships would develop. We had to predict what problems we might encounter and develop theoretical ways of solving them.

How were you supposed to know what issues you would run into while driving 15,000 miles in a used van across the continent for three months? We had to guess at the answers, and then plan all of our costs even though we had no idea what our day-to-day schedule would look like. We didn't know if we would be sleeping in Wal-Mart parking lots for free, campgrounds for cheap, or paying extra for hotels.

Then, we had to decide exactly what route we would drive and calculate all of the statistics that corresponded with that route. How many states? How many races? How many miles? How many people would see our van? The proposal made us think about all of these questions and craft scenarios in our minds. While nothing was concrete, at least we thoroughly considered all of the questions and answers we needed to raise to start the trip.

After the weeks I put in to crafting the proposal and researching potential sponsors, we got little use out of it. We sent it out to a few companies and for one reason or another we just couldn't finalize any new agreements. Most were thrilled with the endeavor despite their inability to lend a hand on such short notice and insisted we keep in touch. Trevor ended up using his own personal contacts and network to obtain just enough support to pull it off.

I was disappointed that I contributed nothing to gathering sponsors, but the proposal wasn't a total waste of time. Just like writing a business plan, it made me think about all the issues we might encounter and how to handle them. It made us plan out our theoretical daily lives on the road. It made us consider the potential crises we would face so we might be able to prepare for them. What's more, it forced us to think up creative ways to exist from a van, and kindled our excitement for the whole trip. It brought out worries and fears, but it was better to bring them out months before the trip than days before when there was nothing more we could do.

If we wanted this trip to make the impact we knew it could, we would have to figure out how to engage people on the journey. The trip may have started out as something we needed to do for ourselves, but it quickly grew into something more. We realized we could use our experiences to show others how they could break free from the cookie-cutter lives that society tends to force upon people.

We wanted to show the world that it was not only possible to do something unique and wonderful with your life, but that you could actually jump into the realm usually deemed as "impossible." Surely, it's not feasible for most to just take off on a three-month adventure. However, if we could inspire a single person to step out of their comfort zone in even the smallest way, we could count that as a success.

One of the ongoing marketing projects we planned to employ was photography. I would be taking photos throughout the trip anyways, but the marketing photos would be different. I had to step out of the realm of "normal" photography and create stunning photos that would encourage people to follow the journey, learn about it, and then become inspired by it. Of course, when photos couldn't tell enough of the story, we would be able to write about our experiences. Most of the writing would take place via Facebook posts, tweets, and blog posts. We just needed a place to gather all of our content. We needed a quality website to serve as the core of our travels and experiences.

Trevor had his own website already, which he mainly used for showcasing his race reports and sponsors. It received little traffic because we never put much effort into keeping it current, but it would become a very powerful tool throughout the following months. His website needed some serious updating. In its current state, it was far from serving our needs. The entire thing needed a facelift. I had to revamp it quickly, alongside the multiple other websites I was actually being paid to build and optimize for various clients.

Luckily, I had just started becoming proficient at building websites on my own, without Trevor's help or advice. Now, all of a sudden, I had three or four of them on my plate all at once. I loved building them, but the work was really stacking up. I wasn't sure where I would ever find the time to finish the site for our journey. Still, I knew I had to get it done. My hours were getting stretched thinner and thinner by the day.

The summer tour website needed a branding scheme and a purpose. The website had a logo I built (and was very proud of) a year prior, but it had a youthful look that didn't match Trevor's largest sponsors. It stood out like a sore thumb among the recognizable, bold logos of Audi and Specialized.

I completely discarded the year-old logo, proud of it as I was. I created a new logo composed of some free-hand mountain peaks and bold, easy-to-read letters spelling out "TrevorDeRuise.com."

The website would still need to be all about Trevor and his racing, but we also needed visitors to understand and be inspired by our incredible journey. It needed places for information about the trip, photos of our travels, and blog posts about the ridiculous challenges we were facing. It had to serve as a landing strip for all the content and photos we would send flying around the Internet. If it weren't for the marketing know-how I had acquired through my projects with Blü World, the project would have been a mess. It would have had no goal, no organization, and no strategy.

This was more than just a road trip, and it needed to be treated as such. We wouldn't be taking it if it weren't adding value to our lives. It had to be profitable, and therefore it had to gain the interest and attention of the public to be profitable.

What we were doing was so far beyond *just* a road trip. It was one more stepping stone on the path towards the high caliber success we sought. This trip was worth a lot, and we had to take advantage of that value. We had to make it mean something, and not just to ourselves.

Marketing the trip was an invaluable part of the planning process. I felt confident we had the project handled with the website, social media, and graphics that I had printed for the outside of the van to direct traffic to the new website. For a brief moment, it felt like that part of the project was *done*, but when is marketing ever done? I should have known better. I was far from done.

I was delivered an impossible task in the shortest amount of time imaginable when Trevor proposed that I capture the trip through video. I was well versed in photography by now, but video was an animal I usually chose to stay far away from.

The few times I had tried to take video with my DSLR camera, I found that there was little I could do to make my footage look better than your standard iPhone video. I was light years away from creating professional videos, but professionalism was what we demanded of ourselves with all the projects we tackled. This would be no different. Whether I liked it or not, I needed to learn to become a videographer. Since we wanted to produce an interest-building video before our departure, I needed to become one in a matter of about three weeks.

I tried to film every chance I could for the first week. I filmed anything I could think of that might be useful for the video, not really knowing what I might end up using. Scenes of grass blowing in the wind and close-ups of the spinning gears on Trevor's bike made their way into my camera lens.

Once I had enough clips and we had a story line down, I had to learn how to edit video with only two weeks left. I remembered how long it took to teach myself how to use Illustrator when I was learning the art of graphic design. That struggle now looked like an anthill compared to the mile-high list of new skills that video editing required.

Learning Illustrator well enough to create professional designs took many rigorous months. The platform had been similar enough that my Photoshop skills helped make the transition fairly smooth. Premier Pro, the video software I now had to learn, was nothing like Photoshop or Illustrator. None of my skills transferred. What's more, I had days rather than months to transform myself into an expert videographer.

I knew I could do it if I believed I could. This was something new and invaluable that I was discovering about myself. I just had to decide to succeed at something, and I could. Not in the magic "ask the universe for what you need" kind of way, but through some newly developed motivation and determination. There was no quitting or giving up any more.

When I was learning to use Illustrator, I was a very different person. I was willing to give up easily. I was not motivated to put in that much work for a reward I didn't fully comprehend. It just felt like a senseless struggle. But that was almost two years ago. The rewards of hard work were not obvious at the time when I was putting in the effort. Twenty months later, I can clearly see the results of my labor.

I spent every spare second of my life for the following two weeks figuring out how to edit all the random clips I had filmed. My computer came with me everywhere. I did not close the video-editing window on my computer screen once while I worked on the project for days on end. I had to find or create extra seconds every day to work on the video. There was no longer time to make lunch, check Facebook, or call my parents.

This is the kind of effort it would take to make the trip possible. Actually, it takes the same kind of effort to make being an entrepreneur possible, too. You have to give up a lot of little luxuries just to make room for work. Then, when the work becomes rewarding enough, it stops feeling like work and anything you had to give up to get there becomes more than justified.

The day before we left, the video was only hours from completion. I may have given up more hours than I wanted to dedicate to it, but the end product was well worth the effort. I was even impressed with the way the video was coming along rather than just satisfied. While I never had any intentions of becoming a videographer, I turned myself into one nonetheless.

Call it obsessive compulsive, but I love to save the best for last. Whether it's with food or my to-do list, I deal with my least favorite things first and work my way through until my favorite is left. I did that with planning this trip as well. My final project was going to be fun *and* relaxing, which was a much welcome concept during my busy summer-semester class and work schedule.

All I had to do was sew and install curtains for the windows in the van so that we could sleep in it in urban settings without curious strangers peering in. It should have been a simple, weekend-long project incapable of producing stress. I did not need any more of that.

I planned on hanging the curtains using 3M Command hooks – plastic hook on one side, adhesive backing on the other. I could stick the adhesive hooks to the plastic interior of the van, which meant the van wouldn't suffer any damage, keeping the resale value high. Then, I would sew elastic loops to the corner of each curtain (which were more like rectangular cloth panels) and loop the elastic around the Command hooks. This way, we didn't have to permanently install anything in the van we didn't plan on keeping for very long.

The hooks are only meant to hold a pound or less, so the fabric had to be light enough that the hooks wouldn't be yanked off the van interior. It also had to be heavy-duty enough that outsiders couldn't see in while we were sleeping.

I found a thick but lightweight fabric that would work perfect, and I bought it in a bright neon blue color (because that color was cheapest). Picking fabric was the only easy part of making curtains, I soon found out.

My first bad idea was not testing the Command hooks. Not only did they pop off the plastic interior of the van when I looped the elastic of the newly sewn curtains around them, they practically jumped off if you looked at them the wrong way. Command hooks would not work, no matter how light the fabric was.

My next bad idea involved suction cups. Since the Command hooks simply wouldn't stick, I figured sticking suction cups to the glass (rather than the plastic around the glass) would provide a tighter hold. I bought the suction cups and put them in place before I realized the flaw in my plan. With the suction cups in the corners of each window, I left about an inch and a half around all sides of every window exposed. I never even had a chance to figure out how to attach the curtains to them. Suction cups were out.

I went back to the adhesive idea, but retained my plan of sticking things to the glass rather than the dull plastic. Sure that this would work, I bought a roll of industrial strength, adhesive-backed Velcro. I stuck one side of the Velcro to the window itself, and the other to the corners of each curtain panel. Aside from a few slivers of light peaking through on the edges, the windows were fully covered with neon blue cloth. Finally, something worked!

At least, it worked for a few hours. It only took one day of baking in the not-that-hot springtime sunshine for my plan to fail once again. The melted Velcro pieces had slid inches from the tops of the windows and left behind a slimy residue that resembled glossy, oversized snail trails.

This curtain project was driving me insane. Trevor liked to remind me that the project should be easy. I wanted to remind him that I wasn't an upholsterer. The curtains would have to wait, and wait they did. They waited right up until three days before we left for our trip because I dreaded finding an appropriate solution.

It was Trevor's ingeniousness that saved the day, anyways. He opted for drilling small screws into the plastic at each window corner, and we wrapped the elastic corners of the curtains around them. We were not sure how long the curtains would hold up, but they would have to do. Those ridiculous neon blue curtains…

In the month leading up to the trip, amongst all the website building and videography chaos, I had to prepare Blü World Inspired and all of our clients to thrive throughout this trip. I couldn't exactly take a three-month hiatus from work. Most of the time I didn't even get weekends off. This trip wasn't a vacation; it was quite the opposite. Blü World was coming with us and we couldn't compromise any of the integrity, work quality, or superior client relations we had built to make it successful. I needed to maintain professionalism leading up to and throughout the trip. This meant that no work would be sacrificed just because we were on the road. I wanted to ensure that our clients would remain unaware and unaffected no matter how ridiculous our circumstances got while we were away. I reorganized all of my to-do lists, computer documents, reminders, and email folders. I made sure that we had a trustworthy assistant remaining in Reno to tackle our billing. Running Blü World from the comfort of Reno was a handful. Running it from the road could turn into an impossible task if we weren't prepared.

I knew that we would need access to Wi-Fi most days of the week, except maybe on the weekends when the majority of our clients were closed or chose not to work. We would spend a lot of time at Starbucks, and when no Wi-Fi could be found, we planned to set up hotspots on our phones.

For the most part, no one needed to even know that we were on the road. If someone was calling, the phone would be answered.

If an email was received, it would be tended to that day. It would be tended to that *hour* if possible. No amount of van camping would keep me from getting work done in a timely manner. Clients with whom I held weekly phone meetings with would, of course, have to know about our plans. We would be driving through large "dead-zones" that could cause us to reschedule appointments if we couldn't get access to phone and Internet service that hour.

While our clients were actually excited to hear about the adventure we were tackling, I was still nervous. How capable would I really be in completing all my work on time with so much unknown lying ahead? It would get done, but at what cost?

As the weeks dwindled down and our takeoff date approached, we had to decide what was coming with us and what would have to stay. There were the items we hoped to bring, and then there were the items that we needed to bring. An ice chest, for example, was one of the most essential items we needed to bring on our trip. A collection of DVDs, for example, was not. The sticky notes I used daily were not. A blow dryer was not.

We were forced to choose an air mattress and hand pump over our spine-saving, memory foam mattress pad. The pad was too big and space was limited. We had to forgo the warmth of sleeping bags in favor of two thin blankets because the blankets also saved room. There was so much to leave behind. Many of the things we originally wanted to bring just weren't going to fit. Here's what made the cut:

- Bikes, spare bike parts, and bike equipment because this was a mountain biking journey, after all.

- A 50-pound stationary trainer for the days when no trails were available and workouts could not be skipped.

- Computers, iPad, iPhones, and multiple charging devices for all of the above because we still had to work almost every day.

- DSLR camera, camcorder, tripod, microphone, extra batteries and chargers for the above because now I was a photographer and a videographer.

- Small ice chest (or over-sized lunch box, depending on your perspective), two-burner stove, one pot, one pan, and four canisters of propane because we had to eat and eating out every meal for three months would both break the budget and our belts.

- The "Canz" – a small wireless speaker in case we wanted music while we worked. Or in case we got sick of listening to each other breathe in the close confines of the van.

- Two camping chairs, a table, and a netted tent, because no one likes mosquitoes and we especially didn't like them while working. This was our bug-proof, portable office.

- A small battery and power inverter to charge all of our many accessories and gadgets.

- A portable solar panel to charge the battery with.

- A solar shower, in case we were unable to find a real shower.

The only other things left to bring were small items like clothes, wallets, soap, toothbrushes, etc. Otherwise, that was all we really needed to live out of a van for three months. So much stuff I thought I *needed* every day was not on the list. But the truth was, I really didn't need more than that. It is so easy to complicate life with unnecessary, excessive things. It's not until you have the opportunity to take a step back that you see the beauty in living more simply. Of course, I don't mean to say that life would be simple while on the road.

Only two things remained to do the night before we left. We had to move the mountain of camping, work and cycling gear from our garage into the van. Then, we had to say goodbye to our goofy, smile-inducing puppy, Ralph.

The weeks leading up to the trip, I squeezed our dog tight every time he came near me. I was trying to will him to understand that we weren't leaving him forever. I wanted him to promise not to be sad or miss us. I couldn't handle it if in a week from now I got a call saying he was acting depressed.

We dropped him off with Trevor's parents that evening, and found no easy way to say goodbye. I played with him especially hard, slipped him a few extra treats, and hugged him too many times. Hot tears trickled down my cheeks as we pulled out of the driveway without our little boy. He had no idea how long we would be gone, but I did.

We spent the rest of the night packing the van tight as if it were a Tetris game, where no hole could be left empty. I split my time between packing and studying for my final exam in the morning. I had been so busy the past three weeks with my four-hour-a-day summer class and video editing that I put off packing until the last minute. I was hoping my bags would fill themselves while I looked away. Of course, they remained empty and I had to either pack them myself in a frantic hurry or leave them in Reno.

Everything I determined I would need to live out of a van for three months fit inside three bags. I had one small sports duffel bag full of regular clothes and one spare pair of shoes. I filled a drawstring bag with my bike clothes and helmet. Last, I had a backpack for all of my work equipment plus all of the necessities I would normally carry in a purse. I felt extremely under-packed. Yet, my three bags looked like an oversized, lumpy mountain of cloth when I set them alongside everything else in our driveway. It all needed to somehow fit inside the already-cramped van.

I left Trevor to putting the final pieces of the van puzzle together, feeling like I was spending more time being in the way than actually contributing to the task.

When I awoke the next morning, I was thinking more about my final than anything else, and it wouldn't hit me that our trip was starting until we were well on our way. I said goodbye to our house and walked a mile to the university. All I had with me was a pencil, a financial calculator, and my phone. Everything I normally carried to school was either packed or had to stay at home, because I was leaving straight from the test and spending the rest of my summer in a cramped van.

The final was a blur. I was more concerned with finishing fast and leaving Nevada than I was about double-checking my calculations. When I finished, I nearly bolted out of the test room, knowing Trevor was already waiting at the main entrance of the school. I found it hard to walk the half-mile to the spot where the van waited and our trip started. I settled for running only when I thought no one could see me, and then continued to run even when I knew they could. It didn't matter what anyone thought. They didn't know it, but we were finally *leaving*.

Part 2 – The Struggle is Real

Embrace Discomfort - Sierra

With my summer class and final exam already forgotten, we began the trek across Nevada in the late morning on June 5th. We had a long sixteen hour drive ahead of us and less than forty-eight hours until the first race in Vail, Colorado.

To say the least, the trip started out in a frenzy. I had to finish the video in a matter of hours on the drive. After all of the time I had put into it, I still hadn't gotten it done the night before our departure, which was when we had planned to blast it out on all of our social media channels. Instead, I now had to finish it on the road and then we would have to stop for Wi-Fi somewhere to upload it. If we didn't upload it that night, we would miss our deadline, which was not the way we wanted to start things off.

We also still had to find dinner and a place to sleep in Utah somewhere (presumably). The next day, we were to finish the drive to Colorado. We would have to find a place to stay in Vail that night, and then get ready for the race early on the morning of the 7th.

Ideally, we would never plan to arrive at a race venue the day before such a huge event. If anything went wrong in transit, there was a chance we might not make it in time. Or worse, we would make it with so few hours to spare that Trevor was nowhere near prepared to race. But since my final exam was held two days before the first race, there was nothing else we could do.

I allowed myself to enjoy the start of our journey for about an hour. It was the first time in weeks that I found myself unglued from my computer screen and the pages of my finance textbooks.

I let myself breathe. All of the planning, packing, stressing, and worrying was done.

Now, the van was plummeting eastward down I-80 at seventy miles per hour. The casino skyline quickly disappeared behind us. Soon, the homes and businesses faded. The few trees that marked tiny patches of civilization became sparse. It wasn't long before we were deep in the grand, empty expanse of the Nevadan desert. It would be an eternity before we were back.

Not long after my respite had surfaced, I had to bury it. Today was departure day, after all, and our "departure video" wasn't quite finished. I estimated that I only had about two hours of work left on it. Ideally, that would be plenty of time to ensure its completion before we stopped in Salt Lake City for dinner and Wi-Fi.

I snapped myself out of the unusual state of peaceful relaxation and switched resentfully back into work-mode. I pulled out my computer knowing that the quicker I finished the job, the sooner I could get back to enjoying the sights out the window and the quiet in my brain. Unfortunately, both my body and my computer had different plans for me. It didn't take more than twenty minutes of staring at my screen for the onset of carsickness to arrive. Of course, the first time I was carsick in years had to be then. The intense concentration I was forcing upon myself must have sent my body into the uneasy plight. Not wanting to be unproductive, I tried my best to ignore the discomfort.

My computer was only interested in making matters worse. Premiere Pro, the editing software I was running, was getting slower by the minute. My small laptop had just enough power to allow the program to work effectively for basic editing. The more clips, sound pieces and effects I added to the video, the slower it got. As I neared completion, the video was a massive file, causing the program to run infinitely slow. I felt like it was adding extra slowness just to spite me and my queasy stomach.

After staring at the screen for another hour, I acquired a painful headache that begged me to stop working. The strain of focusing on a foot-wide screen while the world blurred by in my peripherals was overworking my mind. We had plenty of time before reaching Salt Lake. I could have taken a break, but despite my aching head and stomach, I chose not to close my laptop. I had been working on this video nonstop for the past three weeks. If I was going to take a break, it was going to be because the video was finished.

After nearly two hours behind the screen and with a now screaming head, I finished a masterpiece. I had put so many taxing hours into this project, and now I could *actually* close my editing screen. I was going to celebrate by starring out the window and worrying about nothing for a few more hours. As I tried to empty my mind, it dawned on me that this uncomfortable way of working (literally on the road) was going to be typical for the duration of our journey. Completing projects under less than ideal circumstances was going to be the norm rather than the exception.

I didn't have the cushioned swivel chair, large desk, and distraction-free workspace I was accustomed to. I was temporarily giving that up in favor of a stiff passenger seat, my lap, and carsickness. I just hoped that the amount of work I had to do while physically on the highway was small.

In order to stay on track and get to Vail with enough time the day before the race, our stop in Salt Lake City was brief. We found a Chipotle for dinner, indulged, and then found a Starbucks to upload the video. We spent about an hour at Starbucks frantically replying to emails and taking care of minor projects before continuing on our way.

With darkness freshly upon us, we hoped to travel another several hours before stopping to sleep. There was no civilization for hours, so we weren't sure where we would eventually retire for the night. The last thing I remember was passing through the only town on the map between Salt Lake and Grand Junction, and wondering why we didn't stop. After an hour of fighting sleep and thinking I was winning, I awoke with confusion as the van slowed and then parked.

Trevor informed me that we would be sleeping at a rest stop. You know, those little pullouts on long highways? They usually have a gross graffiti-filled restroom, some picnic tables, and vending machines. *Was it even legal to sleep here?*

As we got out of the van to brush our teeth, we noticed one man bundled in a sleeping bag on the sidewalk in front of his car. At least we had the curtains to cover our windows so no one would know we were sleeping inside the parked van. If anyone was going to get questioned for staying the night at a rest stop, it was that guy. At least, I hoped it was that guy. We had no budget for police run-ins.

I groggily laid out the air mattress on the floor of our sleeping area and discovered it was about eight inches longer than the width of the van. We hadn't realized the van was so skinny. My arm and back muscles ached as I hand-pumped the air mattress up with my eyes still half-closed. After pumping for an eternity, the mattress started to arc up in the middle, compensating for the van's lack of space. *I guess that means it's done.*

As we crawled onto the air mattress and tried to get comfortable under the thin blankets, two things became apparent. One: I only fit if my head was pressed up against one side of the van and my feet were flat against the opposite side. Two: Trevor, being taller, did not fit at all. He either had to sleep with his hips and knees bent, or he had to sleep diagonally and on top of me.

At first the situation seemed silly. It was like trying to sleep in a child's bed. Once I realized what this meant, it wasn't so silly anymore. It meant that we weren't going to get a good night's sleep for the next quarter of a year. There was no way I could sleep with Trevor's knees jutting into my thighs all night. But there was no way he could sleep without stretching out once in a while. I hoped I would just be too tired to notice or care.

Unfortunately, the aches of discomfort kept me awake despite my concrete-heavy eyelids. During my quest for sleep, I realized that the mattress was nowhere near filled with enough air. Any effort by Trevor or myself to rearrange our limbs resulted in a crater forming in the center of the mattress due to extra weight and then us rolling into each other. It felt like trying to sleep in a human-sized taco where we were the rice and beans smashed together in the bottom.

As if finding a comfortable position wasn't enough trouble, the night was unnaturally chilly. Maybe it was just because we had little more than sheets to cover us through the frigid night. In my half-awake state I wished someone would hand me a sweater and some socks so I could fall back asleep. Instead, I felt like I spent the entire night battling the cold that seeped in through every stitch of blanket. I pulled my arms inside my shirt for extra protection from the chill and willed Trevor's sleeping body to be a warmer heat source than it was. Though I longed for more sleep, I was relieved when the sun began to light up the fabric of our handmade blue curtains. Sunlight meant warmth. Sunlight also meant it was time to drive.

We woke to find that our sidewalk-sleeping neighbor was already gone, and we had no tickets stuck under the windshield wipers. I still wasn't sure if sleeping in the rest stop was legal or not, but it didn't matter because we weren't spending another minute there. We were Colorado bound within the same minute that my eyes had opened.

It wasn't long before we crossed the Colorado border that the trip began to feel very real. Utah is just Nevada's neighbor, but Colorado felt new and exciting. After several hours of driving through some of the prettiest country and highest mountains North America has to offer, we arrived at GoPro Mountain Games in Vail, right on schedule. Trevor checked in for his race in the early afternoon, leaving plenty of time for him to pre-ride the course and for me to explore the event's festivities.

GoPro Games is a huge, weeklong event with dozens of outdoor sports, classes, and games. There were over a hundred booths set up, and I was content with picking up free handouts whenever and wherever I could. When I found the "dog-section" of the expo, complete with free dog treats and games for your pup, I couldn't help but miss our little guy. I had never been without him so long and it was only just the beginning.

With so many other things to worry about, the feelings of missing Ralph were buried quickly. Afternoon turned into evening and my stomach rumbled in angry protests. I tried to remember what we had even eaten the past two days. Other than the Chipotle dinner our first night in Salt Lake City, we'd had bananas and some almonds that we had brought from home. Oh, and the free samples of random things that I found at the expo that day. We really needed something substantial.

Lodged in the back of my mind was a fuzzy memory of packing tamales and all the ice from our freezer at home into the small ice chest we now had in the van. I had completely forgotten about the tamales that Trevor's mom insisted we bring with us. I opened our ice chest to find a bag of foil-wrapped deliciousness and a shallow pool of water.

The plastic zippered bag containing the precious food hadn't been shut all the way, so our tamales were soggy with lukewarm water from the melted ice. Trevor assured me that the tightly packed corn meal kept the meat inside preserved and safe to eat, even though they weren't cold. He'd had them camping before, he thought, and insisted we wouldn't get food poisoning. Either way, we were too hungry to really care.

Now that we had our newly discovered dinner on the menu, we needed to find somewhere to set up our camp stove to cook it.

In a fancy resort town like Vail, you can't just whip out a cooktop anywhere you please. Well, technically you can, but people will assume you're homeless and steer clear of you before notifying the authorities. That was not the way we wanted to kick things off, especially since we were wearing sponsor logos all over our bodies and thus had a reputation to uphold.

We weighed our options and decided that the best we could do was to cook from inside the van in a Safeway parking lot. We parked in the corner of the lot, trying to remain inconspicuous, as we fired up our two-burner stove and plopped our soggy tamales into our only pan.

We were trying to be quick and nonchalant, not wanting to be noticed. So when Trevor asked me to hand him something to flip the hot tamales with, I momentarily panicked. We didn't pack any utensils! Aside from the pot and pan, we didn't bring any cooking related items. No forks, no plates, and definitely no tongs or spatulas. As I gave Trevor a wide-eyed look, he immediately understood our dilemma. Without saying a word, I ran into the Safeway and asked for two plastic forks, trying to hurry back to the van.

The only person who seemed to notice our curious behavior was a quacking (yes, like a duck) homeless man who walked by with his shopping cart full of belongings.

"Quack, quack. Quack, quack," he let out every few seconds as he walked by.

"At least we aren't *that* homeless," I said to Trevor when the man was out of earshot.

We tried to devour our tamales just as quickly as we had cooked them. I certainly never imagined having to eat my dinner in secrecy during this trip, or ever for that matter. What I really wanted was to be able to sit down at a table and eat. I wanted to reach into a fridge and pull out a bottle of hot sauce. I wanted to enjoy my food, talking and laughing with Trevor throughout the meal.

Instead, I used a plastic fork to shovel hot-sauce-free tamales out of a pan and into my mouth. Instead of a chair and a table, we ate from the carpeted floor of the van. Instead of the delicious tamales we anticipated, we silently swallowed bites that were outrageously hot on the outside and still cold on the inside. I had to admit, I was already a little homesick. Actually, homesick wasn't even the right word. I was just uncomfortable.

Up until then, I think I was expecting an experience more like a very drawn out camping trip. I imagined my mom's charcoal-grilled meals and my dad's roaring campfires. I imagined card games and picnic tables. Those kinds of trips were all about having a good time, being comfortable, and relaxing. But those trips also didn't produce the rewards we were looking for. The purpose of our adventure was not to relax, *at all*. In order to really make a difference in our lives, we had to accept the discomfort. We had accepted that our travels would not be easy. *Easy was never something we asked for.*

With our bellies finally full of some unhealthy but substantial food, we headed back into the Safeway (complete with Starbucks inside) to work for the rest of the night. This *was* what I expected from the trip – working inside Starbucks for hours on end. I kind of liked this part of the trip. It felt less "homeless" than secretly cooking dinner in a parking lot.

As we walked across the lot to the store, we noticed that a lot of the vehicles in the parking lot were race vehicles. Since they were also parked on the outskirts of the lot, we assumed they were planning to sleep there. Sure, there were ornery "No Overnight Parking Permitted" signs everywhere, but maybe they were making an exception for travelers to the event. We planned to work at Starbucks until 9:00 p.m. or so, and then head out to the van to sleep for the night. In the morning, we could go inside to buy breakfast and get coffee to fuel up for the race.

As the night went on, the store emptied out. The Starbucks closed. All the vehicles we thought were staying the night in the parking lot gradually left. We began to think that maybe the "No

Overnight Parking Permitted" signs were not to be trifled with. If we could just find a Wal-Mart, we knew they would allow overnight camping in their parking lot. Vail itself is too high class to have a Wal-Mart, but our smartphones said there was one only fifteen minutes away in the next town. We said goodbye to our temporary Safeway-Starbucks office and headed to Wal-Mart, eager to get some sleep before the big race day.

Unfortunately, not *all* Wal-Marts allow you to spend the night in their parking lots. Of course, this Wal-Mart in an overly expensive resort town was one of these rare exceptions. We circled the lot in frustrated disbelief of all of the threatening "No Overnight Parking" signs that lined the lot. Now getting tired and irritated, we pulled out our phones to see if there *was* anywhere we could spend the night without the police being alerted. There wasn't. If you wanted to sleep in or near Vail, you had better be willing to fork out a few hundred dollars for a hotel. I wondered how that quacking hobo managed to get by.

We needed to get to sleep soon and we weren't going to break the bank for a hotel room. There was absolutely no budget for that. Instead, we found a highway rest stop another ten minutes down the road with signs everywhere reading "No Overnight Parking Permitted." We had to take our chances. If the police showed up, we would say we were travelers who had been too weary to continue driving safely on the highway.

This sort of "van camping" was not what I originally had in mind. When we talked about VanLife in the months leading up to the trip, I pictured pulling off onto a dirt road, and parking under a picturesque tree with no one else around to notice us. I didn't picture parking next to the smelly bathrooms at a noisy, crowded rest stop, not knowing whether or not we were breaking the law. We hurriedly brushed our teeth in the shadows of the lot and pumped up our air mattress once again. This time, I made sure it was nice and firm. "*No taco mattress tonight,*" I thought. We bundled up, remembering the cold from the night before, and settled in. Before sleep finally took over I was paranoid, thinking every noise I heard would turn out to be a cop knocking on the van doors.

Even with the firmer mattress and extra layers of clothing, sleeping was a challenge that night. I had semi-conscious dreams all night of police breaking into the van to arrest us. Trevor shook uncontrollably from the cold.

We woke up in the morning to find we had no parking tickets and we did have all of our toes. While Trevor hopped out of the van to use the restroom, I slowly pulled myself out from the useless blankets and into the chilly morning air. I opened the blue curtains and made eye contact with an old woman peering shamelessly through the window and into our cluttered living quarters. "*Yes, I slept in here,*" I glared back at her. I wasn't sure whether to laugh or feel embarrassed. We were starting to look a little homeless, I'll admit.

My hair was in tangles and I was living in men's T-shirts instead of the pretty, flowery things I liked to adorn myself with at home. I couldn't help but be jealous of all the women walking around at GoPro games that day. They had their hair brushed, their legs shaved and moisturized, and their outfits were flattering.

I wondered what people really thought when they saw us going about our van-life days. We carried our backpacks around with us most of the time, since they carried our wallets, computers and, in my case, a camera. Trevor's face was beginning to grow scruffy hair, and I was hiding my blonde ponytail shamefully under a hat in an attempt to look less filthy. I hoped that lathering on more deodorant would continue to hide the fact that I hadn't showered in three days.

It didn't help that Trevor and I both look more like high school students than college graduates (or soon to be graduates). Maybe people thought we were runaway teenage vagabonds. But did it even matter what others thought? If we were in the business of caring about the opinions of others, we would be back at home lounging on the beaches of Lake Tahoe and talking with friends about which grad schools we were applying to. *An important part of pursuing your passion in life is ignoring the opinions of others. Hold strong to your vision and don't be derailed from the judgments of your peers.*

As dirty and awkward as I felt, I had to ignore my personal struggles. I especially had to ignore them on this very hot morning while Trevor was getting ready to race. I was already sweating and was about to spend the next hour and a half baking in the sun at 9,000 feet above sea level at the water station on the course. My job would be to hand Trevor a fresh bottle about every twenty minutes as he started each new lap.

This was what we had given up comfort for. This trip wasn't going to be pretty, or luxurious. As I said before, it was by no means a vacation. There was a lot of hard work to do – work we wouldn't feel like doing under certain, inevitable conditions. We had only a small taste of it now, but it was enough of a taste to remind me that the struggle was going to be a long and challenging one.

Embrace the Highs and Lows - Trevor

The beginning of the 2014 season had taken me to one of the greatest highs my young career had ever reached. While my preparation and training had been interrupted several times throughout the winter and early spring due to school and my other responsibilities, I was still stronger than I had ever been. On top of this, I had two amazing bikes, a new confidence going into my second year as a pro, and some great people in my corner supporting and encouraging me.

Right up until the day we left, I won almost every single race I entered. All across Nevada, California, and Oregon, I was feeling unstoppable. While the caliber of these races wasn't quite at the level of the Pro XCT's I would be contending over the summer, there were some very heavy hitters at each of my early season races. I was beating guys who do nothing more than train and race for a living, and it felt great. Even more, it showed me that I could do the same. I could be one of the top names that bike companies fought over.

I had a solid two-month streak of nothing but wins. I won hill climbs. I won down hills. I won cross-country races. I was on top of the world. Also, the prize money began to add up and took some of the pressure off our financial situation as we approached our departure date in June.

Being so new to the cycling world, I will admit that I've always had some confidence issues. Making the jump to the professional level so quickly left me questioning if I was really ready for the elite level of competition. On top of that, making a huge push to be a top professional and race the most prestigious professional mountain bike series in North America didn't help.

However, as the wins began to stack up I started to feel worthy. I started to feel like not only was it okay for me to dive right into the pinnacle of American mountain bike racing, but that it was actually where I belonged. Still, like my history with motorcycle racing had taught me, stepping up to the next level is *never* easy, especially as you near the top. Shortly after we pulled in to Vail, Colorado for GoPro Mountain Games I was abruptly reminded of this lesson.

When we arrived in a drizzly Vail, the caliber of riders who were at the event was immediately apparent. Amongst the masses of spectators and fans were trucks and tents from the top bicycle manufacturers in the industry. The village was filled with booths, banners, and demo areas from the best international outdoor brands.

Amongst the crowds we continued to see some of the biggest names in American mountain biking mingling with fans or heading out to take a few practice laps on the course. While I had raced many of them at one point or another at smaller venues, seeing all of them in one place and knowing that I would be at the bottom of the food chain come race day was a little intimidating.

Beyond the caliber of riders, the course was another challenge with which I was struggling. The tight and technical style with absurdly steep yet short climbs was something I really hadn't prepared for. I was used to races that started out with a twenty or thirty minute climb, followed by a ten or fifteen minute descent. Both were long enough that only a steady and conservative amount of power was necessary to put into the pedals.

On this new type of course, there was no time for being conservative. With hills only lasting one or two minutes, every single one became a sprint. Once at the top, it was then a drag race to keep your position before the next technical section. The outrageously high efforts plus short recovery time in between was something I had never worked on but now needed to learn very quickly.

I've never really experienced nerves or butterflies during the hours leading up to a mountain bike race. While these emotions used to plague my motorcycle career, they have yet to show up since I traded in the motor for a set of pedals. Still, when I rolled through the festival in Vail, I felt as though I *should* have been nervous. Instead, my various van-induced aches and pains dictated my emotions.

My neck was killing me from the cramped space we were sleeping in. I still hadn't fully regained feeling in my toes which had completely froze in the frigid mountain air that crept into our makeshift bedroom in the middle of the night. And to top it all off, the first two nights of severe discomfort had limited our sleep to only a handful of hours in total. Surely we were going to have to toughen up and get better at this whole "VanLife" thing in order to survive the summer. However, I had bigger problems as race time approached, which consisted of eighty of the continent's best mountain bike racers and a course on which I was less-than-comfortable.

With an hour until my start, I waited at the staging area, unsure of how they would call riders into the starting shoot. I knew with how tight and technical the course was, having a good start position would be extremely important. To my dismay, I realized they were calling riders up based upon their amount of UCI points. These are the points that international professionals earn by contesting and finishing well at races sanctioned by the Union Cycliste Internationale

(UCI), the chief governing body of global pro cycling. Can you guess how many of these points I had? None. I wasn't even called to the line. Instead, I was simply allowed to roll up behind the tightly organized group. With a dead last start position, I really didn't have a clue of what kind of lung-bursting agony would await me once the race started.

As we took off up the first hill after the gun went off, I maybe made up ten positions before I had gone so far beyond my own fitness capabilities that I was seeing stars. In a daze and gasping for as much oxygen as I could find in the thin mountain air, I made up a few more positions as we zigzagged up the ski slope.

When we reached the highest elevation point on the course, we had about a mile-long descent before the relentless climbing attacks would start again. I tried to pull myself together and get my heart rate and breathing back under control. I was riding like a zombie. My entire body was on fire with the huge amounts of lactic acid that had accumulated in it from our first short trip up the mountain. I was bouncing off of trees and rocks and doing everything I could to just keep rolling. The final stretch of the descent was a fast and steep section through a grove of aspens with a manmade rock garden at the bottom. With my mind and body in an acidic fog, I took a terrible line into the rocks and slashed my front tire.

Just like that, the first stop on this near-impossible summer tour came to an end. With it went all of the confidence and the high that my early season success had brought. While this was just one of many races to come, it was a huge wakeup call.

The life of a professional athlete is filled with so many ups and downs it's almost comical. Surely, I struggle to find the humor after being thrown (sometimes quite literally) to the ground for the umpteenth time. However, as long as the fire burning within me remains, and I am able to pick myself up again and look back at the years of adversity, it's hard not to smile.

While action sports like mountain bike racing may have more severe highs and lows, this roller coaster is part of life for anyone who chooses to take their destiny into their own hands. Even something as seemingly simple as opening the small business of your dreams will bring extremely trying times that will define who you are. It is during these instances of hardship that you realize what is really important in your life.

If the struggle is worth it and you can continue to wholeheartedly fight for your dream, then you know you've truly found your passion in life. The feeling of incredible satisfaction that comes when you are finally successful after picking yourself up off the ground countless times is one that is strictly reserved for those willing to risk it all for a life fueled by passion. However, the curious thing about success is that it is not a destination that one can reach and then be finished. *Success is a journey.* After every win awaits a new battle and how we continue to fight and grow is what ultimately defines our success.

One of my favorite entrepreneurship professors from college always told me that *if you're going to fail, fail quickly.* That day in Vail, I certainly failed. I needed to figure out exactly what I had failed at, though. I needed to figure out if I had failed because I just was unprepared for that *style* of racing or if I was unprepared for that *level* of racing. If it were the latter, it would be in my best interest to fail quickly, cut my losses, and head home before we continued on this very expensive journey. My bank account would continue to drain and I would never reach my goals if I kept finishing at the back of the pack every week.

It was a huge decision and a difficult one given the circumstances. I was devastated to start things off the way I did at GoPro Games, but I needed to objectively scrutinize what had happened and make an enormous, career-altering choice of whether or not to continue. I had to push all emotions aside and honestly ask myself if what had happened that day was a fluke, or if it would be the story of the summer. Since we really didn't have anywhere to stay that night, I needed to make the decision that very same day. As I fixed my wheel in the parking lot and tried to weigh the options,

I had a tough time analyzing the situation without my emotions getting the best of me.

Sierra has a certain way of calming me down in situations like this. She convinced me to forget everything for a couple of hours and enjoy the festival with her to clear my mind. While I was reluctant at first, it was just what I needed.

The atmosphere and talent at the event was absolutely incredible. Mountain biking was just one of the many sporting competitions that were taking place over the weekend on the mountain. There was kayaking, rock climbing, fly fishing, slack lining, even yoga going on at various locations around the village. The world's best in a wide variety of sports were all there to enjoy the cool mountain atmosphere and to compete in front of the entire outdoor industry.

By far, my favorite event at the entire festival was the "Dock Dogs" jumping competition. You've probably seen this on television. The owner stands at the end of the dock and throws a small buoy up into the air over a small lake or pool. The dog will stand about thirty feet back until signaled and then they will charge to the end of the dock and dive through the air in pursuit of the toy. The dog who jumps the farthest, wins.

These dogs were amazing. They would launch themselves into the air and never take their eye off of the floating target delivered by their trusted owner. There was one very young, black lab that just looked athletic. He was extremely lean and nimble with obnoxious muscle definition that could be seen under his shiny black coat. The dog was noticeably faster than all of the others every time he would take off down the dock. Once he would reach the end, though, he would hesitate just slightly and the massive jump the entire audience was expecting from him would come out as nothing more than a clumsy prance into the water.

This went on several times and the crowd seemed to quickly lose their excitement for him the more he came back up to the dock for another run. When the announcer called for all final jumps, my clumsy favorite only had one more chance to show what he could do.

I thought about myself being in that position. The dog seemed to have all of the potential in the world, he just couldn't seem to put it to use. With only one final shot, I imagined the pressure and anxiety that I would be experiencing had it been me.

"*Don't blow it,*" I remember thinking to myself as if it were I about to make the final jump. "*This is your last chance.*"

Still, the dog looked no different waiting for his owner to throw the buoy. He was still trembling with excitement and using every ounce of his strength to fight back his urges to just run and dive straight into that shimmering pool before being signaled. The competition really meant nothing to him – he just loved the activity.

When his owner finally threw the buoy and signaled to the dog to fetch it, he exploded down the dock. This time, rather than hesitating and stumbling into the water, he unleashed the biggest dive we had seen all day. It was absolutely enormous and was a solid ten feet longer than any of his competitors. The only problem was he took off a few yards before the end of the dock. The result was an enormous splash landing in the exact same spot he had gracefully pranced into each time before.

While that happy young lab went on to finish close to last in the competition, I knew he had laid down the biggest jump of any canine there. The dog still could not have cared less. To him, the only thing that huge jump meant was a few fractions of a second less to get to his favorite buoy in the fun pool.

Surely, last place finishes would never be conducive to building the career and legacy that I am looking to create. However, what was so inspiring was the incredible talent that this dog had, which was fueled solely by his love for the pool. If the love and simple enjoyment for fetching had not been there, it's safe to say this incredibly athletic dog would never fly through the air like he did on that overcast day in Vail.

He had more than a few things to learn before he would ever win one of these events, but that would come with experience. All of the fine details necessary to be successful in this competition could be learned. It was more than apparent that once he was able to time his take off a little better and not become overly excited by the masses of people watching, no other dog would even be able to compete with his jumps.

What this dog had that made him so special was something that could not be learned. What he had could not be instilled upon another dog even after a lifetime of training. What *this* dog had, was passion. And that's what we had in common.

That energetic pup helped clear my mind of the clouds of negativity that had entered after my race earlier that day. I realized that how worried and stressed I was over whether or not I would be able to put in strong finishes at these huge races was actually taking away from my love of riding. I had already proven that I was worthy of being there on that starting line. I had been doing it all season long before this race. However, the sheer size and caliber of the event had gotten to me so badly that the first sign of adversity had me so absolutely filled with doubt that I considered giving up.

Dead last finishes like my new, four-legged friend would not suffice, but I needed to relax. I also needed to continue on with the journey, and have some fun racing my bike. I think Sierra knew all along that this is the conclusion I would come to. I knew deep down that she believed in the journey and wanted to see it become a success.

That afternoon we loaded the bikes and tools into the van and got back on the road. This time, the drive would be short as we only headed about an hour east on the highway to the summit of Vail Pass. At nearly 11,000 feet, the rest stop atop this pass would serve as our home for the night.

It hadn't stopped raining since we had arrived in Vail and the moisture continued all the way to the top of the mountain we now resided at. The winds also began to kick up and I made sure both Sierra and I kept our phones on and near to check for weather warnings. At this kind of elevation, even in the summer, things can take a turn for the worse very quickly.

As the sun set, we brushed our teeth just outside of the van, listening to the constant rumble of idling semi trucks before starting to set up our air mattress. As I dozed off next to Sierra beneath the thundering sound of rain against the van, I wondered what kind of weather we might wake up to.

The next morning we were awoken earlier than we had planned by the vicious roar of seventy-mile-per-hour winds and sheets of rain. The horizon was just beginning to glow from the rising sun that had yet to show its face. With at least another hour and a half of mountainous driving ahead, I decided to get the show on the road immediately, taking only a second to admire the beautiful alpine setting that was getting drenched outside the van windows.

As we got back onto the highway and tried to rub the sleep out of our eyes, the rain quickly started turning into snow. Only ten minutes into our descent down the other side of Vail Pass towards Denver and I had to slow to thirty miles per hour as I fought for visibility out of the ice-covered windshield.

Sierra was still in the back seat of the van rolling up the air mattress when I asked her to come back up to the front seat and buckle up. At the time, I tried to keep my mild panic to myself, but the increasingly treacherous road conditions had me fairly nervous. My white-knuckle grip on the steering wheel only got worse when I touched the brakes and the entire van began to shake and tremble.

I kept reassuring myself that it was just a side effect of the ice and water that were pouring down. However, I couldn't help but feel like this was just a sign of my biggest fears regarding my used van coming true. I threw it into second gear and slowly cruised through the storm, refusing to touch the brakes unless absolutely necessary. Once we got below 7,000 feet the snow had stopped and only a mild rain and heavy winds remained.

Sierra seemed unaware of just how severe my panic had gotten during the intense parts of the storm. She also seemed unaware of the potential mechanical issues our silver home could be facing. Honesty is definitely important in a relationship, but I was almost glad that she hadn't caught on to either of these things. It made me feel as though perhaps I was just overreacting and everything was fine.

As we approached Denver, I put the van back into "drive" and started picking up speed while pumping the brakes a few times to test them out. They still seemed not quite right, but they were far from the shaking mess I had met on the pass so I was partly relieved. Just as one weight was partially lifted off my shoulders, an even larger one was thrown on.

Almost simultaneously, both of our phones began to vibrate furiously and make a terrible screeching noise. With the wind and rain still going strong, I asked Sierra to read me the message that was brightly flashing on both of our screens.

"Emergency alert. Take shelter now…" she read aloud before becoming too entranced with the severity and unexpectedness of the message. Once her words stopped, I looked over and watched her silently mouth the rest of the alert with extreme concern in her eyes. I knew immediately what it meant – *Tornadoes.*

In disbelief and still filled with nerves and excess cortisol from the frightening descent from Vail, I first thought maybe the alert was for somewhere much farther east. After all, tornadoes don't happen in the mountains, right? Unfortunately, after you descend Vail Pass, that *is* the end of the Rocky Mountains. The only thing on the other side is hundreds and hundreds of miles of flat. Our location, combined with the incredible storm that we had been battling all morning was actually a perfect recipe for tornadoes and no amount of wishful thinking was going to change that.

I took the next exit I saw from the highway and we sought shelter in a packed Starbucks. This was not your normal, overly crowded Starbucks though. Most of the people standing inside were not there for a drink. Instead, they were all soaked from the rain and staring down at their phones just as Sierra and I had been doing when we received the alert. These people were doing the exact same thing we were – attempting to seek shelter. This realization made our very first tornado scare that much more real and more terrifying.

We had run inside with our backpacks, not sure if the van was going to be ripped to pieces by a tornado or not. We passed the time in our new Starbucks shelter by getting some work done in an attempt to take our minds off of the chaos that was taking place outside.

For four or five hours, I worked on different blog posts and nutrition articles for TrainerRoad while Sierra designed some logos for clients.

While still enjoyable, this type of work is usually very mundane. I can only tolerate writing for one, maybe two hours tops before I need to get outside and ride my bike. However, given the circumstances, Sierra and I both seemed to seek refuge within our work. It was our escape from the stressful reality inside of that packed coffee shop.

We both seemed to dive into our various tasks with more focus than ever before and I think we had the nerve-racking series of events that took place that day to thank for it. Challenges and difficult situations have a way of filling you with anxiety and stress. Essentially, these are just very powerful motivators that biology has provided us with so that our early ancestors could respond when faced with an angry lion or approaching forest fire. Anxiety and stress are what stimulate the "fight or flight" response within us in order to survive.

In modern life, we rarely encounter "life or death" danger that really requires the stress and anxiety that we build up. I can't say what a caveman felt like before he went to battle with a wild animal, but biologically speaking it was probably a lot like what we, the modern humans, feel like before we go up to give a big speech or struggle to meet a really tight deadline. The difference between the caveman and the modern human is that the caveman had to act on his stress or perish. In today's world, we rarely *have* to act on our stress. We can run away from it. We can avoid it. We can hide from it. However, by doing these things, the stress tends to build up and wear us down. If we always run away when the going gets tough we can never accomplish our biggest goals.

I've always welcomed stress and pressure. Surely, the drive down from Vail that morning had me on edge. My heart rate was through the ceiling from the moment we woke up atop that mountain. However, things were completely out of my hands. All I could do was drive as safely as possible and make the best decisions with the available information in order to keep Sierra and myself safe. Then, we both took all of that extra stress and energy and directed it into our work. We took something that most would view as extremely negative and did the best we could to turn it into a positive.

Stress and anxiety are very powerful. They can beat you down or they can build you up. It really just depends on what you do with them. A life dedicated to passion is sure to come with more stress-inducing challenges than a traditional, "safe" route. *Realizing this and embracing the stress as a motivator rather than an inhibitor is vital.*

Fortunately, Starbucks slowly started to clear after several hours, suggesting the danger was beginning to pass. Sierra and I both seemed to come out of our computer trances at the same time and notice the now slow drizzle outside.

We were headed to Colorado Springs to spend a couple of days training and working with some friends of ours that reside there. Now only about an hour and a half away, we were both thrilled to reach our destination and finish off what had become a very eventful day.

About ten minutes down the highway from the Starbucks we were at, traffic slowed to a crawl. While the wind was mostly finished and the rain was just a minor sprinkle, the aftermath of the storm that had just blown through was devastating. Parked cars with their emergency lights on lined the sides of the road, covered with huge dents and cracked or shattered windows. On the shoulders and on the median laid the culprit of the damage – golf-ball-sized hail by the bucket load.

While the danger had surely passed, it was very clear that had I not found that Starbucks when I did and instead just kept driving, that road-trip-ending hail surely would have greeted us just moments later.

I've never been a big believer in luck. Still, all morning I couldn't help but attribute the way the journey had started out to bad luck.

It seemed like things just kept going wrong that were completely out of my control. As I drove through the hail-laden aftermath on the highway, my self-pity immediately disappeared. We had just dodged a huge bullet and for no apparent reason aside from good-old-fashioned luck, and definitely not the bad kind.

Once in Colorado Springs, our friends Ian and Rachel greeted us with a comfortable bed and warm shower. Ian is actually one of the two cycling friends mentioned earlier in the book who had gotten me into the sport in the first place. After taking a job in Colorado, he left his motorcycle behind and relocated to the 'Springs, taking his long-time girlfriend and adventure partner Rachel with him.

Somewhat of a cycling mecca, Colorado Springs is home to the Olympic Training Facility and more professional endurance athletes than almost anywhere else on earth. The trails are world-class and so are many of the local athletes that use them every day. Of course I wanted to catch up with my old friend, but I also wanted to get some high-quality training in on the hundreds of miles of trails that started right from Ian's garage.

Fueled by the struggle and disappointment of GoPro games just a week before, I quickly fell into a routine at Ian's home. Sierra and I would wake up bright and early and actually cook a real, healthy breakfast (quite the opposite of what we did during our first few days of VanLife in Vail). Next, Ian and I would ride from his door-step and he would show me a different trail or loop to ride before he left for work.

Kyle, my coach, would always email me my workout schedule at the beginning of the week. I would tell Ian what was on my work-out menu for the day and he would find me the best terrain for it. For example, if I needed to do three, ten-minute hill-climb repeats, he would bring me to a long and sustainable climb that he knew would last me at least ten minutes.

After Ian took off for the office, I would head out and get my pre-scribed workout in on whatever fun and exciting new trail he had shown me. Once the riding was finished, I usually headed back to

Ian's where Sierra would be in the middle of a phone meeting with a client or deep in thought over a project. When she saw me get back from my ride, we would start making lunch and take a quick break from the world around us to enjoy time with one another. Following lunch I would usually nap or stretch before we would begin cooking up a hearty dinner in Ian's kitchen. Finally, it was off to bed nice and early so we could start it all over again the next day. It was as if I was finally living life like a professional cyclist was supposed to.

I could get used to this routine. For the first time, life seemed almost simple. My sole responsibility was to become a faster bike racer and nothing more. On top of that, I had everything I needed to make that happen. Sierra also shared in this feeling regarding her own work. Without school, travel, or planning for a huge race tour, she was able to slow down and really give her projects the whole-hearted attention they deserved.

On top of all of this, we had the simple luxuries in life back. Things like a warm bed, a shower, and a kitchen had only been missing from our lives for a handful of days. Still, life without them proved to not be easy. *As I had learned early in life, the price of progress is often great.* This journey was sure to be the greatest price yet, but would the progress we made also be the greatest? Only time would tell.

As the short stay with Ian and Rachel neared its end, we braced ourselves for the road ahead. The next stop would be Boulder, Colorado, for some filming for TrainerRoad. After that, we would be heading up into Montana for my first Pro XCT event. Next, we'd be looping around through Idaho to film two more courses before heading back down into Colorado for another Pro XCT.

We had struggled with only four days of VanLife and now we were gearing up for weeks of it. We needed to toughen up both physically and mentally. We needed to take all of our struggles from Vail and learn from them. Really, we needed to embrace the chaos of life on the road.

Be Persistent - Sierra

I wasn't sure if I was more excited about getting on with our journey or nervous about leaving the comforts of the home we were in. I was going to miss the warmth of the bed, the availability of a daily shower, and the spacious kitchen and fridge. The memories of freezing all night and not having a place to cook food had nearly faded, but were still fresh enough that I wasn't looking forward to facing similar scenarios any time soon.

Discomfort had engulfed us by the time we left Vail. I was tired of blowing up an air mattress every night. The sun and my skin had gotten into a dispute in the high elevation that left my arms, legs, and face redder than a tomato. We weren't eating real food because we had nowhere to cook it. Life was just plain *hard*.

Leaving Colorado Springs meant that we were going to face all of these challenges again, and probably more, for much more than four days. I wasn't sure what that was going to look like for us.

However, being back in the van and on the road was exciting. We weren't dirty or smelly, our ice chest was full of ice and food, and we had had a few really good nights of sleep thanks to our temporary refuge at Ian and Rachel's. Positive vibes were at a definite high.

The delight didn't end when we arrived in Boulder. Before we even worried about where to spend the rest of our evening, we explored the downtown area. This would be one of the only times during our trip that we would find ourselves in a town worthy and capable of being explored on foot.

Unfortunately, playing tourist doesn't last long when you have hours worth of work to catch up on. We found another Safeway to spend the evening working in. Actually, we didn't just find a Safeway, we found the *coolest* Safeway ever. This Safeway had an entire wall of gluten free foods rather than your typical bay's worth. (Did I mention that Trevor and I both eat exclusively gluten-free?) It also had a sushi bar. Have you ever heard of a sit-down sushi bar inside of a grocery store? Neither had we, and it was incredible. We kept saying things like "You know you live out of your van when grocery stores excite you."

That was where the excitement stopped. We weren't in Boulder to explore or sightsee or enjoy the grocery store sushi bar. We were in Boulder to film the first two courses of our trip. We had about eleven of these to do in the next eleven weeks.

We spent two hours that night just figuring out how to set up all of the GoPro cameras around the outside of the van. Once we figured out where on the van to even mount them, we had to tilt them all properly so that their wide-angle lenses didn't see each other or the van in their peripherals. Each adjustment was so small, it took ten tries of moving and overcompensating to get the shots right.

With all of the camera housings and attachments positioned and ready to film, we marked their places on the van with sharpie dots and took them down for the night. We found a Wal-Mart parking lot to sleep in (that allowed overnight camping), and prepared to get up with the sun to start filming.

When Filming Day Number One finally arrived, we tried to prepare the best we could. Trevor's job would be to drive a steady and constant thirty miles per hour during the entire course. My jobs were piled high. I had a course map to read, so I could tell Trevor where to turn. I had five GoPro remotes with blinking lights to watch because they would tell us if a camera stopped recording and allow me to turn it back on with the push of a button. I also had two GPS devices, which would track our position, elevation, and speed throughout the course. We had two just in case one malfunctioned or died. Finally,

I had a notepad and pen that I would use to record any incidents along the course such as turnaround points, stop signs, etc.

The sun wasn't even above the horizon when we arrived at our starting location. We set up the cameras according to the marks we had left on the van the night before. I went through and made sure the shots still looked good on each camera. Trevor connected five, twenty-foot long cords from each GoPro, through the windows of the van, and into a power inverter plugged into one of the van's DC outlets. Next, he taped down all of the cables to prevent them from blowing around in the wind. Lastly, he threw a large magnetic sign on the back of the van that read, "CAUTION. SLOW MOVING VEHICLE." This brightly colored sign was our feeble attempt at not angering other motorists as we inched our way down their highways going twenty to thirty miles per hour under the speed limit.

With the setup done, Trevor handed me the iPad, which contained the maps that provided our turn-by-turn directions. He was ready to go, and asking which way to turn out of the parking lot as I fumbled with the map. It was a hand-drawn PDF and had no scale, mile markers, or anything to gauge distance. I could tell where our first turn was out of the parking lot, but after that, I had no idea how far it was until the next. All I saw was chaos.

Trevor assured me that it couldn't be that hard, and I wished I could trade him spots. As we approached every intersection, I strained to see road names in time to tell Trevor whether he was turning or not. Then, after each turn, he insisted I tell him how far until the next one. I struggled to write down the time of each turn on our notepad (which would make editing the footage easier), keep an eye on the blinking lights on the remotes that signified all of the cameras were functioning properly, make sure Trevor kept his speed consistent at thirty, and estimate the distance to the next turn. I needed a team of four people in the back of the van, but I only had myself.

When I thought the map and navigation were my biggest issue, the cameras started shutting off randomly. I couldn't watch the red, blinking lights every second of the drive, so when I looked back down to check them and saw only four blinking lights, I momentarily panicked. But all I had to do was push the "record" button to get them going again.

When the first camera went out, pushing the record button didn't help. I tried to sound calm in my frustration, but Trevor couldn't believe that I managed to screw up such a simple task. All I had to do was push a button, right? He was stressed from having to drive thirty miles per hour in the shoulder of a bunch of two-lane county highways. People blew by us on blind hills and corners, often putting themselves and us in danger. We had to pull over to fix the camera since apparently I couldn't do it with the remote. But the camera hadn't just stopped recording; it shut itself down entirely, which severed its connection to the remote. While I was relieved that I had done nothing wrong (yet), this meant that the cameras could all potentially fail for no known reason.

Forty miles into our fifty-five mile course, they did just that. One after another, each camera shut itself off. We had to pull over, turn it back on, and then we might make it another mile down the road before the next one shut off.

As if the cameras weren't stressful enough, I managed to get us lost. We drove down a certain road for too long, but we never saw a sign for the road we needed to turn on. After we doubled back, we realized the hand drawn map used a different name (County Road 10) than what was written on the street sign (Fox Hollow Dr). I was biting my nails, trying not to throw the flashing red remotes in frustration. Filming was turning out to be a nightmare.

Clearly, we had some kinks to work out before our next course. Unfortunately, we didn't have time to prepare because the second we finished filming the fifty-five mile course, we had to go back out and film the one-hundred-and-ten mile course next. We allowed the cameras and remotes to charge using the large battery inverter and solar panel we had with us. At least *that* piece of technology seemed to work. We also spent almost two hours uploading all of the footage from all five cameras onto our external hard drive. There was so much footage, each memory card took about twenty minutes to transfer and we quickly realized our 1 TB hard drive was not going to be big enough.

The second course of the day was just as convoluted and confusing, but twice as long. The only thing I got better at was estimating the miles between each turn on the map.

We finished the second course in a little over four hours. Between the seven hours of driving/filming; three hours of setup and tear down; two hours of charging and re-prepping all of the devices and cameras; and four hours of transferring footage to our hard drive, it turned out to be a sixteen-hour workday. We hadn't physically done much, but the lack of sleep, hours of travel, and constant stress wore us out.

Working on the road was shaping up to be harder than I expected. Half the time our basic needs like food, water, rest, and shelter weren't even fulfilled, and still we had our work obligations to honor. We would have to get used to working hungry, tired, and smelly because our situation wasn't going to get any easier. It was clear anything that could go wrong, probably would. We had done so much to plan and prepare, yet it seemed to make no difference.

You could blame this solely on unfortunate circumstances, but we knew it wasn't. *Surprises and constant challenges simply come with the territory when you wander off the beaten path and into the unknown.*

After spending several hours in a Peet's Coffee shop, we excused ourselves from work for the rest of the night. We settled down with a laptop and an iTunes movie rental in the back of the van in the Wal-Mart parking lot in Boulder. After such a demanding day, watching a movie was about the only thing we had energy left for. We would be up bright and early again the next morning to start on the two-day drive to Missoula, Montana.

Remember to Enjoy the Journey - Trevor

After the never-ending day of filming, it was almost a relief to get back on the road to drive peacefully towards Montana. We had nearly twenty hours of driving ahead of us until we would arrive in Missoula for the Pro XCT. Still, this was a welcomed task compared to the thought of setting up another GoPro or driving thirty miles per hour down another tight and bumpy farm road while angry motorists blow by going seventy.

After a small meal from our new favorite Safeway, we hopped in the van and headed north. The trip started out rather uneventful. First, we left the mountains of Colorado behind. Then, we blazed through the entire state of Wyoming, admiring bison and historical landmarks like the battlefield of Custer's Last Stand from the highway. Once the sun went down, it began to rain and I decided to pull over at a rest stop at the Montana border to stay the night. The next morning, it was still raining, though not as hard.

After another eight hours of driving we reached Bozeman, Montana. With only a few more hours to go until Missoula, we were making great time and I decided to reserve us a campground just outside Bozeman. Though it was still raining, the campground provided showers, Wi-Fi, and some much-needed peace and quiet compared to the rest stops and grocery stores we were used to.

When we woke up the next morning, the rain had finally stopped and an enormous rainbow spanned the snowcapped peaks just to the west. Sierra cooked up some eggs while I made coffee and we relaxed in the cool Montana air. For the first time since starting this trip, we found happiness and contentment while living out of the van. While our circumstances were far less luxurious than they had been just days prior at Ian and Rachel's house, we were beginning to get the hang of this whole "VanLife" thing.

Once we finished up our breakfast in the mountainous wonderland we were privileged enough to call home for the night, we hopped in the van. With the last short leg of driving ahead of us, we were both excited to arrive in Missoula and get the weekend of racing underway. The van splashed through a few puddles on the dirt road leaving the campground before reaching the damp pavement. Once on the highway, the motor roared to life as we got up to speed.

Warm thoughts of the beautiful morning we had just experienced in Bozeman filled my mind as we cruised through the fog. I looked to Sierra to see if she too felt the sudden swing in our fortune. To my surprise, the expression on her face was that of *sheer terror.*

She was frantically yanking at her seatbelt in an effort to liberate herself from it. Finally, it clicked free and she lunged out of her chair and into the back of the van. Once out of her seat, I was able to see the thick, dark cloud of smoke that had begun billowing out of her door. I immediately jerked on the steering wheel towards the shoulder and skidded the van to a halt on the side of the road. It looked as though I had spoken too soon about our sudden swing in fortune.

Part 3 – Pushing Forward

Do Not Hesitate - Trevor

Planning for the worst, I started thinking of all of the ways we could extinguish a fire if necessary. While I jumped out of the van and ran over to the passenger door, I knew that my ability to fight whatever fire awaited me on the other side of the van would be limited. We didn't have a fire extinguisher and our water supply consisted of two half-full water bottles. If it came down to it, I planned on throwing as much of the damp Montana soil into the flames as possible and just hoping we didn't lose all of our belongings in a fireball aside the highway.

When I got around to the other side of the van, huge white and gray clouds of smoke were billowing out of the door. It was tough to breathe as our lungs burned from the terrible smell of an electrical fire. Fortunately, it did not look as though flames had yet erupted.

I quickly ripped the large plastic panel off of the inside of the smoking door and inspected the internals. Within the hollow metal door was a mechanism for the door handle, a small motor for the window, and the door lock system. Just as I had suspected, it was the power door lock unit that was on the verge of flames.

The smoke appeared to be dissipating as I stared, dumbfounded, into the now gaping hole in the door of my van. I concluded that when I turned the van off after abruptly pulling over, it must have killed the power to the door lock motor and stopped the impending doom that we appeared to be on the brink of.

Once it was clear that we had narrowly avoided the danger, I tried to piece together what could have possibly gone wrong. I knew for sure it was the door lock motor that had almost gone up into flames.

What led me so quickly to this conclusion was something that had happened earlier that morning. As if Sierra was sitting inside playing a trick on me, the door locks kept randomly locking me out of the van while I was trying to load up in the rain at our campground before departing.

On top of this, we had unfortunately discovered a leak in the passenger side of the van, just above the strange weld on the door that I had noticed before purchasing it. It had dumped rain all night before this incident and when we awoke, we realized that there were several streams of water going down the inside of the doors near Sierra's seat. Even today this is still just theory, but it looked as though the leaky doors had allowed one of the door locks to get wet. The damaged door lock motor then shorted-out, ruining the entire door lock system and nearly catching the van on fire.

We were literally seconds away from going up in flames on that desolate Montana highway. Though we had narrowly avoided turning the van into a smoldering pile of melted metal, the damage was still fairly extensive. For starters, none of the power door locks worked. As silly as it may sound, this was tough for me to accept. The van had been my very first vehicle in my six years of driving to have power door locks. Such a simple luxury, but I was pumped on the ability to lock the entire vehicle with the push of a button. While some young professional athletes dream of Ferraris and Lamborghinis, all I wanted was to be able to lock my vehicle without walking around to every single door. I got to enjoy my precious power locks for almost a month before this trying day when they almost literally went up in flames.

After the incident, Sierra's door was stuck shut. As though the intense heat from the near flames within had welded the door closed, there was absolutely no hope of getting it open. Instead, Sierra now would have to climb in from the back of the van or hop across from my door. This made our already inconvenient situation even more of a spectacle.

Lastly, all of the locks were completely unreliable now. Aside from Sierra's door, we could still push or pull the small black knob on each door to manually lock or unlock it. However, sometimes that just didn't work. I could push down the lock knob on a door, shut it, and it would open right back up without needing a key. With almost $35,000 worth of mountain bikes, computers, and cameras in the van, this made for a very dicey situation.

Terrified to turn the van back on and deliver power to any of the electrical devices in the soggy doors, I called my uncle back in Truckee to seek advice. This was definitely one of the perks of having a family member in the automotive industry. I always had a lifeline when it came to vehicle issues. Unfortunately for me, though, there was not much this lifeline could do beyond offering some verbal tips and suggestions over the phone.

I explained the situation to him and he was fairly shocked. Never before had he heard of a vehicle almost igniting while flying down the highway at seventy miles per hour due to a door lock motor. Without being able to check things out for himself, he recommended I just pull the fuse from underneath the dash that delivered the power to the locks. While this didn't fix the set of new and exciting issues we now faced with the van, it did offer us peace of mind that no electricity would be entering the inside of the doors and, therefore, no fire would ignite. Well, in theory at least.

With our heart rates back under control and all of the windows rolled down to clear out any remaining clouds of smoke that still remained inside of the van, we got back on the road. Missoula was only about an hour away and we were ready to get back to the races and have a few days off from driving.

Then, like in one of those bad, comedic movies where the main character is flooded with dramatically unrealistic bad luck, we heard a strange *click* come from inside of the dash. Next, the cool air that was steadily flowing from the air conditioning vents came to a halt. Sierra and I both looked at each other, thinking the exact same thing: *"Really?"*

First the door locks try to kill us, now the air conditioning goes out? Believe it or not, the realization had us both laughing. Unlike the door locks, our broken air conditioning was in no way a danger to us or our belongings. We knew we would probably feel differently about things when we reached the hot and humid East Coast. Yet, for now, we shared a laugh at the absurd circumstances that had been thrust upon us all in a single morning.

Thankfully, the remainder of the drive went without any more surprises. We arrived at the race location at a ski resort just outside of Missoula in the late afternoon. The dark rain clouds began to part as I parked the van, unveiling the magnificent Montana sky for the first time since we had been in the lush, green mountains.

Though we hadn't driven much that day, the eventful morning had left both of us exhausted. I wasn't in much of a mood to pre-ride the course, but I knew I needed to, due to the infamous Missoula "A-line."

At professional events like Pro XCT's and World Cups, race-courses will often have several "option sections." These will usually consist of an extremely difficult, yet faster and shorter "A-line" and an easier, safer, but longer and slower "B-Line." The venue in Missoula just so happens to be famous for one "A-line" that trumps all others on the entire race circuit.

The section is located at the very top of the mountain, just as you start descending back down to the start/finish area. It consists of a massive vertical drop, ten feet down and twelve feet out to a small dirt landing that spits riders out onto a steep and narrow trail. Unforgiving trees and stumps line both sides of the trail, leaving just enough room for a pair of handlebars to plummet through.

The trail just beyond the landing comes in at a sharp, ninety-degree, right-hand turn. While there is a small berm to aid in catching out-of-control riders, the steep hillside makes it almost impossible to slow to a safe speed before slamming into the corner. Any miscalculation on the jump sends riders skidding out of control into the wooded abyss.

With my moto background, I had yet to find an obstacle on a mountain bike course that really made me uneasy. Often times, motorcycle races would have hundred-foot or larger jumps where the consequence of making a mistake could very easily be death. On a mountain bike, the worst-case scenario was usually nothing more than a broken bike or some cuts and bruises. However, the drop in Missoula is *huge*. When I rolled up to it for the first time on that Thursday before the race, I got the same exciting and nerve-racking feeling my dirt bike had brought me so often. With so much vertical free-fall combined with the thirty to thirty-five percent downhill grade that waited below, the stakes were high. Serious injury awaited anyone who miscalculated the massive drop or clipped a tree on the rapid descent.

Still not quite recovered from the travel and stress, I opted to take the "B-line" on my first lap around the course to warm-up more. This alternative route added about five seconds per lap. With a six-lap race ahead on Saturday, the penalty for taking the safer line would be about thirty seconds total. While this may not seem like a lot, thirty seconds can very easily be the difference between a top five finish and a twentieth place finish. In this type of racing, thirty seconds could make or break a rider.

Knowing that I had to take the "A-line" or sacrifice a huge chunk of time, the huge drop began to consume my mind as I slowly cruised around the rest of the course. *One of the most important things that motorcycle racing had taught me regarding these types of situations was not to hesitate.*

If something scared me but I knew it was attainable, then I just had to go for it. Every second spent hesitating allows the mind to fill with more worry and doubt. These negative thoughts begin to build up and will eventually surpass the initial desire and confidence. The more time spent dwelling on the possibility of failure, the more you set yourself up for it. Thus, you are often persuaded to play it safe and left to wonder what could have been.

While there are some instances that require careful speculation, others require you to follow your gut and take that leap of faith. Taking risks is an essential part of progress. Whether it be in sports or business, there will come a point where getting to the next level requires some sort of gamble. *After all, what is the value of success if there is absolutely no consequence for failure?*

Pre-riding the course slowly took about thirty minutes to make it around the tight and twisty trails. Each lap was about four miles in length and ascended about 1,200 vertical feet. After choosing to put off the huge drop for one more lap, I had thirty minutes to think about just how massive it was. My mind filled with all of the scenarios that ended with me being carted out of the woods by the paramedics after attempting it. While I still knew I *could* do it, I started wondering if I *would*.

As I rolled through the final corners before the dreaded section, I felt my palms start to get sweaty. The doubt in my mind was screaming at me to take the "B-line" again.

"Just take one more lap to think about it," my worried mind urged.

Then, just like the moments before takeoff on an enormous motorcycle jump, everything seemed to slow down around me. My hands tightened on the handlebars and I stopped pedaling, allowing my bike to smoothly coast towards the ledge. Subconsciously, I had made the decision to hit the drop that lap. I knew I could do it and I knew I needed to do it. I had never hit something that big on my mountain bike, but I had faith, which overpowered my nerves.

The negative thoughts in my mind went silent as I pulled back on the handlebars and began the free-fall. Narrowly missing trees on both sides of the trail, I instinctively put my index fingers on my front and rear brake levers in midair to prepare for the wild ride that awaited once my tires touched down.

Both wheels hit the landing at the same time, bottoming out my suspension and sending force up through the pedals and handlebars and into my body. Wide-eyed and without a breath, I squeezed the brake levers harder as I skidded my way towards the rapidly approaching berm just below the landing.

Slowing down at all before the corner was out of the question. The speed and momentum acquired from the free-fall, combined with the terribly steep landing, made survival the number one priority in the rapidly approaching berm.

My rear tire was completely locked up and sliding across the damp soil. My front was nearly locked, but broke free every time the tire tread dug into the breaking bumps on the trail. I slammed into the berm, again fully compressing my suspension. Confident my tires could lose traction at any second and throw me into the woods due to the tremendous force, I felt my tight grip on the bars grow evening tighter.

With my heart pounding out of my chest and my arms burning from squeezing the grips so tightly, I skidded out of the berm and continued rolling down the trail in triumphant disbelief of my sketchy success. *I did it.*

It may not have been as smooth as I wanted, but I made it over the mental hurdle of hitting the "A-line." I ridded myself of all of the doubt and worry that had filled my mind just moments before. With a newfound confidence of the section, I immediately went back up the mountain and hit the drop a few more times; each attempt a little smoother and safer than the last.

With the "A-line" out of the way and out of my head, I was feeling really excited for the race on Saturday. Aside from the drop, my legs and fitness had also felt really good during my pre-ride, only adding to my confidence.

It's a strange feeling going from hitting a huge drop on my bike, to writing about nutritional trends while sitting inside of a coffee shop. My life has a tendency of moving, quite literally, at very high speeds sometimes. My work outside of cycling is a way to slow everything down and channel my energy differently. In a way, it recharges me and keeps me fired up and excited every time I get to throw a leg over a bike.

Upon loading up the bikes after a long day of practice, we drove into town and found another Starbucks inside of a Safeway to get some work done. As the sun set, Sierra and I shared a big cup of Safeway soup while utilizing the free Wi-Fi to attend to the various matters that required our attention at that moment.

Just down the road from our temporary Missoula office inside Safeway, was Wal-Mart. Filled with RVs, it was clear overnight parking was acceptable here. With a little peace of mind, we made the lot our home for the remainder of our nights in Missoula.

Sierra and I spent the Friday before the race at Starbucks. Aside from getting in a short TrainerRoad workout on my stationary bike trainer in the parking lot, we remained indoors all day. I needed to rest and recharge before my big event on Saturday and Sierra and I both needed to catch up on work.

When Saturday finally rolled around, I was relieved to feel focused and excited, rather than beat up and haggard like I had at GoPro Games. Being my first Pro XCT, I knew I would have a dead last start position, so I didn't stress over it. Instead, I just went about my normal warm-up routine as I do at every race. Pedaling up and down the highway leading to the ski resort, I went through my various heart rate zones. Everything was feeling exactly the way it was supposed to. From a mental perspective, it was as if I was just at another local event.

As riders began staging, I calmly rolled up behind the pack, accepting my terrible start. While Vail seemed to have *most* of the biggest riders in North America, this Pro XCT had *all* of them. Plus, there was a sufficient handful of international pros. I was unfamiliar with some, but knew exactly who others were from magazines and cycling movies. Still, the predominant emotion I experienced was excitement, not nerves.

The gun sounded and we all took off up the mountain. The first half of the course contained the majority of the climbing and made for a painful start. I did my best to make my way through the pack, often going way over my physical limits just to gain another position.

Hitting the big drop every lap and consistently moving up as the race progressed, I felt unstoppable. On my fourth lap and with nearly 5,000 feet of vertical elevation gain now in my legs, I began to feel the effects of my overzealous efforts from the first lap. I knew I had started too hard, but I wasn't sure what the consequences might be. My excitement had gotten the best of me on that first ascent of the mountain. Patience had been quickly thrown out the window when I began the first climb in last place in the excitement-filled moments immediately following the start of the race.

Now, with only two laps to go, I was starting to unravel. My legs ached with exhaustion. My power began to dwindle, so did my focus. As I made my way up the mountain, one rider after another began going by me. At first, they were barely moving faster than me. By the time I got to the top, though, they were flying by. I had worked extremely hard for the first hour of the race to make my way past so many riders, and now they were overtaking me left and right. I put every ounce of energy I had left in my body, into my pedals. Trying to limit the damage that was taking place, I focused on just *finishing*. It was clear my result would not be what I had hoped, but I refused to let the disappointment that I had experienced in Vail return. A mediocre result was better than no result.

Pushing through, I managed a mid-pack finish. Given my starting position at the very back of the pack, I was actually pumped on the outcome of the race and even happier with the learning experience. The style of course and the style of racing at these professional events were both so new to me. It was almost like learning how to race all over again.

Knowing that I was capable of a mid-pack finish on a "bad day" was a huge confidence booster and filled me with excitement for the next round. Further, I now had a few Pro XCT series points, which is what they use for assigning start positions. If things went as planned, I would have a slightly better start position at the next Pro XCT, a week later, back in Colorado Springs.

As we loaded up the van, I had one word on my mind – progress.

Forgive Yourself - Sierra

If Trevor hadn't been dripping with sweat, I would have hugged him so hard that he would have fallen off his bike. I was relieved that he had finished the race, and on top of that, the result was a great start. To me, that was something to be stoked about. Still, in classic Trevor fashion, there was no time to celebrate. We had things to do and places to go, I understood.

With the race held in the evening, we ended up leaving Montana after sunset. One would think it made sense to spend the night in Missoula at that point, but that just wasn't our style. There would be no spare hours in our schedule for the next week.

We were in the middle of a twelve-hundred-mile loop around the Rocky Mountains, and we had less than a week to make it back to Colorado Springs for the next race. To make things trickier, we had to detour west through Idaho to film back-to-back courses in Coeur d'Alene and Boise.

While the rest of the pro athletes drove back to their Missoula hotels to shower and relax after the strenuous evening of racing, Trevor and I hit the highway. Coeur d'Alene was about three hours northwest of Missoula, not far from the Canadian border.

Even though it was far past dinnertime, Trevor and I both needed to eat something. With no time left to waste visiting grocery stores, our only option was to eat whatever was in the van already. I took inventory of the food we had with us: two bananas, a mostly-eaten bag of grapes, two nectarines, two cans of tuna, almonds, arugula, boil-in-a-bag brown rice, four boxes of quinoa, and six single-serve ranch cups. The CEO of TrainerRoad, someone Trevor greatly looks up to, would have gotten quite the kick out of our menu for the night, as he often teases Trevor for "eating like a squirrel" due to all of the nuts and berries he snacks on. In this case, a homeless squirrel, and I was right there with him.

We immediately scratched the fruit and nut items off the menu because we had been munching on them all day already. We didn't have time to find somewhere to set up a stove and cook, so the rice and quinoa were out. This left arugula, tuna and ranch. The arugula was going to go bad if we didn't eat it and we figured we could add the tuna to it for a little more sustenance.

We pulled off the freeway and onto the dirt shoulder of the onramp, wasting no time to find a more suitable place to have dinner. I quickly jumped out of the van to open and drain the canned tuna, and also to be eaten by swarms of mosquitoes. I skipped around in a small circle trying to dissuade the bloodthirsty bugs from landing on my skin while I poured out the tuna-water from both cans. I got some of the smelly liquid on my foot during my spastic dance, thus ensuring I would carry the fishy odor with me for the rest of the night.

Back in the van, we mixed together our ingredients and attempted to swallow every last bite of our odd dinner concoction. All the while, stray mosquitoes assaulted us, causing us to panic and nearly send ranch-covered tuna pieces onto the van's ceiling. Despite the strangeness of the meal, I managed to polish off my entire plate in a matter of minutes. I had been too hungry to care about details like taste.

We drove through midnight and stopped to sleep at a Wal-Mart in the middle of nowhere, thirty minutes outside of Coeur d'Alene, Idaho. I bundled up in my sweats for the cool night approaching and fell easily to sleep even with my legs bent uncomfortably in the too-narrow van.

When morning arrived, my eyelids flew open. It was bright out and it was so hot inside the van I felt like I was going to die. The heat made the already small van feel like a trap. I was suffocating with every breath. Or maybe I just thought that because being enclosed in heat was my worst fear in the world. *I have to get out. I have to hurry and get out!* I threw the blankets from my body and stripped my sweats off to reveal a T-shirt and shorts underneath. That didn't help at all.

Trevor was still asleep. *How could he be asleep?* More importantly, how was I going to get out? If I opened the side doors of the van, the air mattress would push itself out, relieved to no longer be smashed in a van that was too small for it. Then the doors wouldn't close again until we deflated the mattress. I didn't want to wake Trevor if he wasn't ready to get up. He had just raced the night before and deserved all the sleep he could get. But the *heat* was overbearing. I was starting to panic. It wasn't even that hot but my mind has always had a problem comprehending hot air. It makes me feel claustrophobic, and it has done that for as long as I can remember. I wouldn't be able to calm myself down until I escaped it.

I frantically crawled over Trevor, grabbing my shoes from the front seat. A sleepy grunt escaped him as I squashed some body part of his. I let out a breathy "sorry" as I clambered out the driver's door (since the passenger door was now *stuck* shut) and into the warm morning air.

It was probably only eighty degrees at the most. How was I going to handle sleeping in the van when it was ninety degrees? Or one hundred? I guessed I was going to find out soon. I would really have to suck it up because there would be no relief once we got moving, now that the air conditioning was gone.

After a few minutes of standing aimlessly outside the van, I wasn't sure what to do with myself. It could be another hour or more before Trevor decided to get up. There was only so much time I could kill in Wal-Mart, and I didn't want Trevor to think I was lost or kidnapped when he awoke to find me gone. My heart rate dropped back down to a reasonable level and I decided to get back in the van. I would just have to wait out the heat and test my will power that had entirely vanished minutes ago.

I quickly forgot all about the heat when we arrived in picturesque Coeur d'Alene. The small city sits on a massive, pristine lake surrounded by sky-high green mountains. The lakeshore is lined with tall, luxurious resorts and vast beaches. Beyond the resorts lies a busy shoreline park complete with hundreds of yards of sandy beach. On a hot, blue-skied Sunday, plenty of people were cruising around on bikes, skateboards, and even roller skates.

Unfortunately, we had no time to waste with sightseeing or beach exploring, though I badly wanted to stick my toes in the sand. We had a course to film and we knew it would be an all-day event. We drove straight through the town and pulled into a small parking lot that marked our starting location.

As Trevor mounted the GoPros to the hood, sides, and back of the van, I went around to each one and performed my routine. After completing the process with each of the cameras, all that was left to do was hop in the van and turn the remotes and GPS devices on. *But not everything turned on.* As I pushed the power buttons on each remote, only one of them lit up with life. I tried to recollect the previous night's events. First, we left Missoula. Then we ate dinner on the side of the freeway. Then I plugged everything in to ensure the batteries were all charged while we drove. I remember very clearly that each of the remotes finished charging. I had *checked.* But... did I remember to turn the remotes off after they finished charging?

If left on, the remotes would search for Wi-Fi signals from their GoPro counterparts. With the GoPros turned off, the remotes had nothing to find, so their search would continue until the batteries were dead. I thought I had turned the remotes off. I knew I was supposed to. But it looked like I had only turned off one, and the rest had spent the night searching for a connection that didn't exist before they died.

Trevor and I were both frustrated. We were on a tight schedule and the remotes would take at least an hour to charge. We had parked illegally in a small lot to set the cameras up, so now we had to move the van somewhere it could sit for an hour while we set up our solar panel and power inverter. On top of being angry with myself, I felt guilty for missing such an important detail. It was my job to make sure that all of our equipment was ready for filming. There was nothing we could do now except find a place to park and wait while the remotes charged again. We parked near the lakeshore, so I decided to relieve my frustration by visiting those beaches I was ogling on the way in. *Might as well.*

I was upset about my mistake. While we had endured a lot of hardship already, it's always the most challenging to accept setbacks when you are at fault. As an entrepreneur, though, mistakes are both unavoidable as well as vital. Mistakes are the best opportunities for reflection and growth. Sure, it's frustrating, but it should never be devastating. *Accept your mistakes, learn from them, and move forward.*

As my mind began to unwind and let go, the only thing I had to worry about for the time being was how far into the cool blue water of the picturesque lake I should wade.

Unlike the never-ending filming experience in Boulder, we only had to film one course in Coeur d'Alene. We figured that filming in Boulder had thrown every possible challenge at us, so we were prepared for it all now in Idaho. Luckily, the gorgeous mountain town decided to play nice, and we finished filming with no incidents by two in the afternoon.

When we arrived at the course finish line we were exhausted and hungry from filming. We took the cameras down from the van and I wrapped up the five extra long charging cords as we drove to find lunch. Even without all of the mishaps, filming was a stressful event that required our constant attention for hours. Even the slightest lapse in focus could create an error that was only resolvable by starting over. I thought I would want to go back to the lake and enjoy the gorgeous setting after filming, but I didn't. I just wanted food and sleep. There was no time to revisit the lake, anyways. We had another course to film in Boise the next day before finishing the long haul back to Colorado Springs for the Pro-XCT race the following weekend. Time was expensive and indispensable. We polished off a late lunch in town before getting back in the van and back on the road.

This day was dragging on with no sign of ending, other than the fact that the sun was sinking in the sky. We still had to get all of the footage off the GoPros to make room for filming in Boise the next day. Then, everything needed a fresh charge. With no time to spend at a Starbucks between courses, I had to get this all done on the road while Trevor drove us to Boise, nine hours away.

I sat in the back of the van with my laptop and the external hard drive that was filling up quickly, spending an hour just exporting and checking footage from each GoPro. Once the footage was done, I plugged in as many remotes and GoPros into the van's DC outlets as possible. While everything charged, I found my chance to relax for the first time that day. Had it really been *that* morning that I woke up dying of heat in an empty Wal-Mart parking lot? It felt like days had passed since then.

We drove through town after town in Idaho's high desert, admiring the enormous grain silos and wondering how people lived so far away from civilization. Hours of driving through peaceful farmland punctuated by the occasional home and barn passed. As the sun lowered itself towards the flat horizon, my stomach began to grumble again. We now had almost no food with us, and who knew how far it might be before we came across another gas station. They had become few and far between for most of the drive. Just as the sun dipped below the horizon, we saw a sign to exit for fuel.

Trevor pulled off the freeway and into the gas station, not because I was hungry, but because the van needed gas. I took the opportunity to head into the convenience store to grab some food, only to find the place closed. We would have to settle for eating our last two bananas for dinner and nothing else. As Trevor filled up the van and took a phone call, I enjoyed the ability to walk around. My legs were starting to get a strange numb and wobbly feeling from sitting for so long. I walked in circles in the empty gas station parking lot and tried to guess at what was growing in the farm fields all around us.

I contemplated running off to examine the fields more closely, but Trevor called me back to the van. His phone call was over and we had to get going. There would be no more leg stretching until the gas tank neared empty again.

As we continued down an exceptionally straight highway with nothing to look at but rows of corn and more mystery crops, I struggled to stay awake. I usually don't sleep in cars, usually *can't* sleep in them if I try, but this trip was exhausting. Rather than struggling to get comfortable and trying to sleep, I found my eyelids heavy as lead as I fought to stay awake.

We arrived in Boise late at night (or early in the morning, depending on how you look at it) after our drive from Coeur d'Alene. After spending the night in yet another Wal-Mart parking lot and getting up early, filming was upon us again. The heat in Boise was unnatural in the early morning. We set up as quickly as we could and took off from the sad excuse for a lake, the starting location of the course.

Still mentally exhausted from the previous day's filming as well as the increasingly hot van that we were entrapped in, I had little energy left for Boise. Coeur d'Alene had been a beautiful course, with plenty of scenery to look at. In contrast, the Boise course wound its way through several industrial parks, so I was content with watching the flashing remotes as opposed to the scenes out the window.

I had always thought of Boise as a beautiful oasis of mountains and trees. Not that there weren't mountains, but the city was not what I had expected. It was lacking in foliage and any sign of moisture. It reminded me a lot of Reno, but without the surrounding pine trees and the life-providing Sierra Nevada Mountains.

Maybe Boise was right for the people who lived there, but I could never see myself spending more than a day in the dusty Idaho capital. I wondered if the people who grew up there thought it was beautiful, the way I am accustomed to find tall granite peaks and pine trees beautiful. That's what I grew up with, after all. Would people from Boise think the Tahoe forests were beautiful or did they prefer the wide-open expanses of dirt and rock?

The things I found appealing *had* changed as I moved from one state to another; from one landscape to its opposite. Now, I love my Nevada home and all of the opportunity and growth that it has provided me. Had I never stepped outside of my comfort zone and gave the new location a chance, I would be on an entirely different journey than the one I am on today and I don't think it would be for the better. *Keeping an open mind, wandering beyond what is familiar to you, and looking for beauty wherever life takes you are all valuable attributes of the passion-driven entrepreneur.*

We had been on the road for countless hours in a matter of two days. Trevor hadn't been able to ride since his race two evenings prior. There was no way he could put in another full night of driving and still have functioning leg muscles. Wal-Mart was not an option for a third night in a row. We needed to cook some real food, shower, and Trevor needed to ride. Instead of driving all through the night, we stopped several hours later when we reached a campground in Twin Falls, Idaho.

The tiny campground was such a refuge from life on the road. With laundry going, showers taken, and a real dinner cooked and eaten, we began to feel a little more human. I spent the evening working in my new outdoor office that included a weak-but-adequate Wi-Fi signal and picnic table under a huge oak tree. Trevor spent the evening being questioned by curious passersby as he tried to complete a rigorous TrainerRoad workout on his stationary trainer at our campsite. He really was quite a sight, with his all-red lycra clothing covered in sweat as he struggled to catch his breath atop the bike, eyes fixated on the laptop in front of him. I couldn't help but laugh every time some retired motorhome-driving couple walked by and curiously asked what he was doing, despite the obvious signs that he was in no condition for conversation. The sight had become normal to me, but it was far from normal to everyone else.

When we left Twin Falls the next morning, I checked the map on my phone to orient myself. I wasn't even sure where in the state of Idaho we were or what our route to Colorado would be. I told the map to navigate me to Colorado Springs, just to get a feel for where we were going. I figured we just had to go east through the rest of Idaho and then halfway through Wyoming before heading south into Colorado.

Instead, the route on my phone screen showed that we were heading south into Utah before entering the western border of Wyoming. I don't know why, but I felt uneasy about going back through Utah. Utah was just Nevada's neighbor to me. It felt like we were heading back home.

Why would heading home make me feel uneasy? Shouldn't I be happy to see a familiar piece of land that I connected with? Wouldn't it be nice to drive through recognizable terrain?

I usually find comfort in places that remind me of home. Sometimes it's a tall pine tree that reminds me of the mountains around Tahoe. Other times it's a granite boulder that my childhood self would have loved to crawl all over. Recently, I've even begun to feel at home amongst the desert sagebrush. It is so opposite from the giant oak trees that reminded me of my childhood Northern California home, but it has grown on me since moving to Nevada.

Instead of comforting me, the sagebrush made me want to run fast and far away. We weren't supposed to be so close to home. This journey was supposed to take us to entirely new and far away places, and Utah was neither of those.

Crossing the Utah border made me realize something I hadn't noticed before. I used to be afraid of change and discomfort. I used to love being "home," whether that meant California or Nevada. I needed familiarity to thrive. But this trip was making me crave discomfort. I wanted to see how far we could go and what struggles we could endure. Anything we faced out on the road would make the struggles we had back in Reno seem insignificant.

I didn't want to be back in Utah because we hadn't had our fair share of adventure yet. There was so much more to learn on this trip that was going to change us. *I could feel it.* We hadn't even left the Rocky Mountains yet. We were still in familiar territory and I wanted to be thrown into the unknown. I wanted to test my ability to overcome hardship and change. If I passed those tests, I really was cut out to live my life on this unbeaten path. This trip was my way of knowing for sure if the unique life of an audacious entrepreneur was right for me.

We drove through Utah and into Wyoming that day before finally stopping at a rest stop. Trevor really needed to get another workout in, especially with only a couple of days before the next race in Colorado Springs. A rest stop TrainerRoad ride would have to do the trick, since we didn't have time to find actual trails.

Trevor got out of the van to get his bike from the back while I pulled my computer out onto my lap in the passenger seat. I watched

Trevor walk around the van, swatting at bugs the whole way. Then, before he could open the back door, his swatting became more furious until he darted back into the driver's seat, yanking the door shut behind him.

"There is *no way* I am riding here," he huffed in aggravation.

I would have laughed, but then I realized about half of the swarm of mosquitoes that were attacking him outside were now in the van. Suddenly, his plight was no longer funny, nor did it just belong to him. We both frantically clapped our hands together in the air around our heads, trying to kill the bloodsucking creatures that relentlessly plagued our VanLife experience.

We got back on the road, and drove at least a hundred miles before we stopped again to reattempt the workout. We were at such a high elevation in the southern plateaus of Wyoming, we hoped that mosquitoes wouldn't be an issue. It was already completely dark outside, so we parked under a street light in the rest area parking lot. Trevor managed to finally get his ride in with only a few mosquito bites to show for it.

Even though it was night and we were already at a rest stop, we weren't ready to sleep yet. We still had a hundred or more miles in us, so we got back on the empty Wyoming highway for the third time that day. It would be a few more hours before we found another rest stop for the night.

When we awoke in the morning, I realized we had overslept. It was almost ten and we had meant to be up at least two hours earlier. After hastily deflating the mattress with Trevor's lifeless body still asleep on it, I ran down the hill from where we were parked to use the bathroom. But when I got there, the bathroom was closed. They were doing some kind of construction. Actually, when I looked around, I noticed that *all* the vehicles around were construction vehicles. I looked to the rest stop entrance and noticed it was blocked by a row of bright orange cones.

"Rest Stop Closed," the orange signs said. Upset that I didn't get to use the restroom, I hurried back to the van where Trevor was brushing his teeth.

He looked confused that I had returned so quickly, so I just pointed to the signs and said, "I think we better get going."

We laughed at the ridiculousness of being trapped in a closed rest stop as we squeezed the van between two of the cones meant to keep us out. I was grateful no one had knocked on the van and found us sleeping there. Either the construction workers thought the van was abandoned, or they knew we were sleeping and decided to let us be. Either way, no one called the police on us and we only had a handful of hours left before we would be back in our beloved Colorado.

Build Momentum - Trevor

Ian and Rachel welcomed us back into their home once we arrived in Colorado Springs. Though we were really starting to get a handle on VanLife, it was wonderful to have a shower, kitchen, and a bed that I could stretch out in. Mostly, it was great to be back riding on Colorado's endless trails, rather than desolate parking lots, rest stops, and campgrounds.

Just like during our first stay, Ian was my morning trail guide before he headed to work. This time, he took me to the race location for the Pro XCT that was set to take place the following Saturday. The course wasn't fully marked, but I was still able to get a good feel for what was to come. The terrain at the venue suited my riding style very well.

It's a funny problem for a professional mountain bike racer, but I've always been a little uncomfortable on trails with dense vegetation. Tight trees, roots, and encroaching ferns are not obstacles I usually face back home in the Reno-Tahoe area. With that being said, the wide-open, desert landscape of the Colorado Springs course meshed really well with me.

The fast and dry single track featured a few technical rock sections, some steep climbs, and a lot of cacti. Completely exposed with no refuge from the sun due to the fairly barren landscape, the heat was sure to be a big factor come race day. Also, the venue was located at just over 6,000 feet of elevation. The thin, dry air was almost identical to what I spent my days training in back home. I was extremely comfortable on the course and felt confident after the solid finish in Montana. Oh, and did I mentioned we got to sleep in an *actual* bed for a few days as well? Things were definitely looking up as race day approached.

The Saturday of the race was hot. We headed to the course in the morning and the temperature was already in the nineties and rising quickly. I knew that hydration and mental strength were both going to be key on the desert course. As I warmed up on a dirt road behind the venue, I got to talking with another young pro who was also trying to get his blood flowing. He was from Australia and had made the trip to Colorado for the remainder of the Pro XCT's and the two North American World Cups that were just a few months away.

Talking with him, I realized my struggles were pretty similar to his, from a racing standpoint at least. When it came to VanLife, Sierra and I were in our own realm of misery. Also, talking with this other rider reminded me of one of the things I love most about cycling. It reminded me of the worldliness of the sport. As a professional cyclist, the entire planet becomes your office. With races taking place on almost every continent, a successful career atop a bicycle was sure to take me around the globe a few times.

I've often felt like this is one of the reasons that eventually led me away from motorcycle racing and its limited opportunities beyond the United States. I'm definitely not the type of person that thinks the universe will just serve you up your wildest dreams on a silver platter as long as you *believe*. However, *I would say that intention and knowing what you want is powerful. So is maintaining an open mind when things don't go as planned.*

The reason I say this is because I am now at a place in my life where my childhood dreams are starting to take shape. While they may not look exactly like I imagined they would when I was in grade school, they are everything I had hoped for and more.

I have always had an intense desire for travel and adventure that, looking back, moto would have never been able to fulfill. Even more, I don't want my health and nutrition advocacy to be limited to just one country. I want to take my messages all over the world and even the most successful of moto careers will only take you across the United States. In cycling, it would almost be impossible to build a career in just one hemisphere of the world. The cycling industry and community are so present all across the planet that international exploration comes with the job.

While at the moment, things may not have been very glamorous, as Sierra and I drove a used van across America, I could see my future taking shape. I was starting to see all of the possibilities that were just in front of me. Cycling has opened so many doors of opportunity in my life that I never would have found atop a dirt bike, and the best has yet to come.

We were set to go off at 2 p.m. during the peak heat of the day. While I waited to be staged, I could already feel the sweat pouring down my neck and back.

With a few Pro XCT points in the bank from Missoula, I was excited to finally start somewhere other than dead last. To my dismay, the race just so happened to be the finale of the US Cup Series, which coincided with several of the Pro XCT rounds. Because of this, they were selecting start positions based on US Cup points, rather than Pro XCT points. Can you guess how many US Cup points I had? *Zero.* The takeaway from all of this confusing mountain bike jargon is that my hope of an improved starting position was gone.

So there I was, in my familiar location behind the big mass of incredible cycling talent, waiting for the gun to go off. I continued to remind myself to take it easy on the first lap, having learned the consequences of starting too hard in Missoula. Unfortunately, though, the field in Colorado was almost one hundred deep. I needed to make a lot of passes to have a decent finish, but I wasn't sure how easy that would be on such a high-speed course.

Just like in the Tour de France, when speeds are high in a bicycle race, something called "drafting" comes into play. Think of drafting as geese flying in a "V." The goose in front pushes the wind, thus allowing the geese behind to work less. In cycling, riders will swap the lead position in an effort to work together and allow one another to recover in between huge efforts. By doing so, groups of riders working together are able to go much faster than a lone rider, pushing the wind solo.

When the gun went off, I knew I needed to make my way forwards as quickly as possible. There would be a good amount of drafting going on throughout the race, so moving up would be difficult as riders started working together and the field broke apart. However, I made sure to keep my efforts controlled and calculated to prevent the train wreck I had experienced in Montana.

We started on a very rough, paved road. Speeds immediately reached over thirty miles per hour as the group of riders sprinted up it, just inches away from one another. There was a small crash as we approached the first turn onto the dirt. As a result, the huge group of riders was split and I surprisingly found myself near the front of the pack as we headed out onto the trail.

My brief appearance at the front was short-lived, as a rider went down in front of me just a half mile later entering the first rock section. I got pinned between him and a wall of cacti and rocks and almost went down myself. I scrambled and tried to jump over him, only to get tangled up in his bike. The entire thirty-second debacle put me immediately back into the dead last position I had started from. Even worse, I could see the lead groups, all drafting off of one another and working together as they blazed across the valley below.

At that point, I threw caution to the wind and pinned it. With this style of course and how far back I already was, the only shot I had at a remotely decent finish was if I gave it everything I had from that second on. The next two laps were a frantic blur, as I pushed my physical limits and passed as many riders as I could. The dust burned my eyes and lungs, while the sun kept me on the verge of overheating.

On the fourth lap of the six-lap race, I began seeing some of the riders that had passed me during my struggle on the last laps in Montana. Only this time, it was *me* who was doing the passing. Each time I passed someone, I gained a little more adrenaline and pushed a little harder towards the next.

On the last lap, I no longer recognized anyone from Missoula. I had passed all of the riders that I was battling with in the green mountains and was now in the next tier of riders; the tier that I had fallen short of just a week before. Thirsty, hot, and covered in dust, I continued to make passes all the way until the finish.

In the end, I finished even higher up in the pack than I had in Montana, and I had done so under much tougher conditions. Still far from a win, or even a podium, it was progress, yet again, and I was thrilled.

Sierra whipped me up a celebratory protein shake back at the van while I wiped my filthy, sweaty body down with a damp towel. I had forgotten to bring towels for this type of occasion, but I was absolutely disgusting after the high-speed desert race so I resorted to using the grease-covered "bike towel" I had for wiping bike chains down. Whether or not it helped, or just made me even filthier is still a debate between Sierra and me. However, in the moment, I didn't care.

Things were coming together. We had already faced *a ton* of adversity. But, we had gotten on the road in the first place to turn a dream into reality. A dream that was taking more shape with each race that passed. For sure, things had gotten tough, but no one ever said it'd be easy.

In true VanLife fashion, we would not be headed back to Ian's house after this brutal race to shower and rest. Instead, we would be driving deeper into the heart of America. As soon as my greasy towel wipe-down was done, we were headed east not having a minute to spare. In the span of two weeks, we had three courses to film, another Pro XCT in Wisconsin, and I had recently discovered a USA Cycling (USAC) Regional race in Illinois that I wanted to make it to. A strong finish or a win here could not only earn us some much-needed prize money, but it would also give me USAC points, which would be used to determine my start position at National Championships later in the summer.

Out of the mountains and farther away from Reno than either of us had driven before, we were really on our own from here on out. As the van roared down the highway into the flat, farm-filled abyss, Sierra and I tried to mentally prepare for the next two months of pure, uninterrupted VanLife.

Part 4 – No Safety Net

Roll With the Punches - Sierra

The West was finally behind us. As we ventured into the plains, all new territory and the unfamiliar awaited. I had heard stories of these places where mountains didn't exist, but had never actually seen any of it with my own eyes.

Colorado Springs marked the end of the mountains. After that, there was Kansas and it was just as flat as I had expected. If there had been just one small hill to stand atop to gain perspective, I was sure we would have been able to see the curvature of the earth.

The longer we drove through Kansas, the less the landscape changed. My head became dizzy as my eyes processed unending rows of corn whizzing by at seventy miles per hour. I imagined what kind of life I would live in the middle of Kansas, with no large cities to run to. I imagined what kind of life I would live without mountains. The openness felt vulnerable, as if we could be attacked by who-knows-what from any side at any time.

Living in the mountains had always felt safe. You can only see so far, and if you're out on a hike or a ride, you can always look for the tallest peaks to orient yourself. I couldn't imagine how lost I would get in Kansas, with only the sun to use as a compass.

As we reached the eastern end of the monotonous state, my unease dissipated. Still no mountains, but the roads became hilly and fields of corn turned into thickets of bright green ferns and leafy trees. After hundreds of miles of flat farmland, the rolling green hills were comforting.

We arrived in Lawrence, Kansas in the late afternoon. Had there not been a course to film there in the morning, we would have continued driving well into the night. After finding and parking at a local grocery store, I stepped out of the van and knew we weren't in the West anymore. The air felt sticky. It felt gooey, actually, like it was dripping from the sky above and coating me in a sheath of slime. If I were to have bottled the air, I could've probably drunk it. Humidity was an all-new experience to me, and I was certain I was going to start drowning from breathing it. Beads of sweat turned into drops on my forehead and rolled down to collect in my eyebrows. I imagined droplets of moisture accumulating in my lungs, slowly filling them like water balloons.

Inside the grocery store, I took a moment to truly appreciate the air conditioning. Then, the quest for dinner began. Finding a dinner that was gluten free, healthy, and didn't require a stove was always a challenge. Sometimes we crafted our own salads from bags of lettuce and chopped veggies. Other times, we bought salami, cheese, and rice crackers and pretended that that was enough food for a meal. In the West there had been Safeway, which makes delicious, hot soup you can eat on the spot. We had eaten a ton of it in Colorado and Montana because it was so cheap and filling. Even if there was soup at this grocery store, eating anything hot sounded miserable. We could always do more arugula salad, but that didn't sound like enough.

We explored the deli bar, where we usually found nothing we could eat, until I spotted a heaping pile of plump tamales. I joked to Trevor, "Hey, want some more tamales?"

He lit up. "Yes! Let's get them!" he nearly squealed, eager to end the usually disheartening dinner hunt, and unable to stomach another bite of arugula.

With a response like that, I had to laugh. We ordered eight of them and headed for the grocery store's eat-in café area. We even found Wi-Fi in the café, so we opened our computers to work while we enjoyed our surprisingly delicious dinner.

We spent the night across the street from the grocery store in a vacant lot behind a truck stop and diner. Prepared to film very early in the morning, we headed to bed when the sun went down. The humidity had not let up, and it felt just as hot at night as it did in the blistering afternoon sun. The first few hand-pumps to the air mattress sent sweat dripping from my face. By the time it was full, I wanted to take a cold shower. With no shower available, I had to lay myself down on the sticky, rubber mattress instead. Sleeping felt gross, so little of it occurred that night.

Adding insult to injury, we couldn't even open the windows on the van while we slept inside of our miniature sauna, due to the swarms of mosquitoes that were outside. While the air outside was just as hot and damp, some kind of breeze, no matter how small, would have felt so nice to have. Our first night in the summer humidity of Middle America was absolutely wretched.

I drifted in and out of sleep throughout the night, constantly changing positions or taking a knee to the gut as Trevor also tried to escape the uncomfortable heat. I wanted the sticky mattress to stop touching me altogether, but it clung to my clammy skin wherever it could. When light began to enter the van, so did more heat.

A feeling of utter panic filled my entire body as the tiny space in the van seemed to close in on me like a hot, damp, death trap. I leapt for the door that was curiously already open. Sleepy and delirious, I found Trevor standing outside with no shoes. His panic-stricken face was red and glistened with sweat, as I was sure mine did, too.

I rubbed some life into my blurry eyes and examined our surroundings. No one was around to see our frantic evacuation since it was six in the morning on a weekday in a truck stop parking lot. I wanted to curl up on the patch of grass in front of the van and sleep more. A loud *whoosh* followed by a hissing sound brought me to attention. I turned around to find a zombie-like Trevor releasing the air from the mattress, eager to do away with the awful rubber heap. He looked as haggard as I felt.

I wanted to experience discomfort on this trip for the sake of personal growth, but this wasn't exactly what I had had in mind.

I was thinking more along the lines of mental strife, not relentless, physical discomfort.

Since the sun had abruptly awoken us so early and it was impossible to fall back asleep, we started filming immediately. We finished the two-hour drive around the course before nine in the morning, leaving the whole day ahead of us. We drove to the nearest Starbucks, eager to get back inside and back to work, in the air-conditioned luxury.

We brought all of our GoPros, remotes, charging cables, and the external hard drive into the coffee shop with us. It was much easier to charge everything at Starbucks than while we drove, even though it still took well over an hour to complete the task. Plus, with all of our mysterious electrical problems in the van, Trevor preferred we not charge anything from the van's outlets at all. The risk of something else failing catastrophically in our silver home was much too great, so we had to limit any extra use of it.

While Trevor ordered himself a black coffee, I plugged in our mound of gadgets. The gentleman at the table next to ours openly chuckled at the ridiculous amount of cords and electronics I was laying out. It was as if I was setting up some kind of high-tech workstation suitable for someone in the CIA.

Trevor returned to the table with a coffee and the news that we had earned ourselves a free drink from our membership deal. He only drank plain black coffee, so he insisted I use the reward to get myself a big, fancy, and expensive drink that would otherwise not be within budget. This seemingly miniscule surprise was just enough to change the mood of our early stay in the Midwest. *Many times, celebrating the little things can make the biggest difference in staying positive and enjoying the ride, no matter how rough it gets.*

Once we were done working in Lawrence, we headed northeast to Macomb, Illinois for the regional event Trevor had found just days prior. It took the rest of the afternoon and evening to drive from Kansas to our Illinois destination. As soon as we arrived in

Macomb we looked around for somewhere that might have Wi-Fi. Not long after we entered the town, we exited it without any trace of a coffee shop.

Macomb was a tiny farm town that looked mostly run down. Aside from a Wal-Mart and a few fast food chains, it didn't look like any modern businesses had reached the town or ever would. Starbucks was out of the question for Wi-Fi. A nearby Burger King was our best option. I couldn't remember the last time I had been inside of a burger joint. I felt so out of place and didn't want to stay long because the whole place felt dirty. I didn't even want to set my laptop on the table, not knowing why every surface we encountered was sticky. Instead, I sat in a chair with my computer on my lap, trying not to touch anything.

While we worked inside the smelly Burger King, the dark skies outside suddenly opened up. We watched from the shelter of the restaurant as sheets of heavy raindrops drove down onto the pavement. The wind kicked up, and soon raindrops were not coming from above, but from left and right. Some even seemed to fall upwards. We waited a few minutes for the rain to subside but it only came down harder as we watched. We decided to give up on working and move the van before the roads became flooded leaving us stranded at Burger King.

We walked out the first of two sets of doors, putting us in the restaurant's entryway. As if warning us not to go any further, the rain pummeled the glass doors in front of us. As soon as the wind turned and the rain started blowing sideways rather than straight at us, we made a run for it. I bolted for the van's back door that I now had to use exclusively since the passenger door was still stuck shut, and fumbled to get my key into the keyhole. I was only out in the rain for a handful of seconds, but when I flopped into the van like a fish out of water I was drenched from head to toe.

Before Trevor turned the engine on, we watched flashes of lightning momentarily light up the sky from all different directions. Every time I tried to watch for a bolt out one window, I would spot one out of the corner of my eye in the opposite window.

We drove across the street to the Wal-Mart parking lot where we would sleep for the night. The lightning crept closer. We could see the bolts as they ignited and then blossomed across the skies above us in an amazing spectacle. I couldn't contain my excitement and let out a gasp or a hushed "*whoa*" every time I made eye contact with a bright, discernible bolt.

I had never seen a storm like that in the West, and I wasn't sure if I would see one ever again. I wanted to take in every last bit of it. I photographed it for a while until I felt like the camera took away from the simple beauty of watching the rain fall and the lightning crack without distraction.

This was just one of the privileges that traveling allowed us. We got to see things that no one talks about but are still worthy of their own documentary. The lightning storm was one of a kind. People would travel from all across the country to see it if they could. If Mother Nature could promise a lightning storm of that caliber every night, you bet there would be tourists there to witness the phenomenon. Despite being one of the greatest spectacles we had ever seen, it would never be featured in a travel brochure. Unless you're from the Midwest, it would be so easy to go a lifetime without ever experiencing such a show. *Often times the most amazing things in life are subtle. They are not in the spotlight nor do they receive attention from the masses. Rather, they wait patiently for someone to simply appreciate their humble magnificence.*

I awoke the next morning with a blissful feeling; we had no filming and no traveling scheduled for the day. We actually had a little bit of time on our hands. Not wanting to go back into Burger King, we searched on our phones for other places in the area that might have Wi-Fi. We found one prospect and one prospect only. There was a coffee shop located in the town square, and we had to hope it had an Internet connection.

As we entered the town square, which was literally a square shaped road with a church in the middle, I noticed just how old the town was. Every single building around the edge of the square looked to be at least a hundred years old.

The coffee shop was as charming as the town square itself. It looked to be decorated solely by thrift store and garage sale items. No two coffee mugs were the same, nor were the chairs, nor the light fixtures. The coffee wasn't very good, but at least we found Internet... very slow Internet.

We suffered through the painfully slow connection and got as much work done as we could manage. Neither the coffee nor the Wi-Fi speed was worth staying any longer. After spending a few hours working, Trevor began looking for a place to stay for the remainder of the week. As it turns out, there was a campground on the same lake where the mountain bike race was being hosted over the coming weekend. To our luck and surprise, the campground only charged seven dollars a night; well worth it compared to our other option of sleeping in a parking lot all week.

The campground was huge, well groomed, and on the edge of a large lake surrounded thickly by trees. I couldn't believe they charged such low prices and were able to keep the place so well maintained. I come from California, after all, land of all things expensive and regulated. In Macomb, there weren't even site numbers; just gravel pullouts and mowed-down grass areas. You could park wherever you wanted and simply set up camp.

We chose a spot that was far away from the road as possible where we thought we would have the fewest neighbors. We were approaching the Fourth of July weekend, and the place was going to be packed. Everyone else would be there to take part in the festivities, while we tried to carry out our day-to-day lives in peace and quiet. With our spot picked out and the next five nights of camping paid for, we organized what little camping gear we had. We had a brand new mosquito tent and two camping chairs, and that was really it.

We actually had a truly delicious meal to eat that night. We decided to try something new and throw together a mash up of several healthy ingredients. In our large pot we steamed cubed potatoes, organic ground beef, bell peppers, mushrooms, and green beans. It wasn't exactly a recipe, just a conglomeration of foods that were tasty and hopefully went well together. The result was a mouthwatering dish that felt luxurious by our traveling standards. For once, we actually had too much food and had to force ourselves to swallow the final few bites. We hadn't been full in weeks and we weren't about to throw any food away.

Unfortunately, the longer we sat inside of our bug-free tent and ate, the more bugs seemed to come in. The spiders were the worst. They were of the Daddy-Long-Leg variety with a leg span at least as large as my palm. Every time we turned around, there was a new one crawling up the netting inside of our safe house. Trevor can't stand spiders, no matter how harmless, so he finished his dinner from inside of the van.

We had an entire week off from traveling so I wanted to get ahead on work before things got crazy again. Trevor proposed that we ride our bikes to the coffee shop in town, and I thought he was crazy. *Ride to the town seven miles away? With all of our stuff on our backs?* He wasn't joking. He wanted to leave the van in its spot to both mark our campground and to save gas. Besides, riding was good for us and we finally had that kind of time to spare.

I threw my heavy backpack with laptop, camera, and plenty of equipment onto my back and tried to make it lie comfortably on my spine.

With Trevor riding in front to break the wall of wind, the journey into town really was easier than I expected. Most of the ride was entirely flat, so we just had to get a good pace going and stick with it. My legs were starting to burn when we arrived at the same, quaint coffee shop we had found the day before. We worked, drank coffee out of old, mismatching mugs, and then rode the seven miles back to our bug-filled campsite.

We had purchased two nights worth of the same dinner, so we indulged in our new favorite meal of ground beef, potatoes, and vegetables for a second night. After we ate, I caught Trevor staring deeply into the distance, but not because he saw something. The look on his face was one I recognized. He was thinking about something that bothered him or worried him, and I wasn't sure if I dared ask. I didn't have to.

"What else can we do, David?" he asked me when he noticed me watching him. (He has called me "Dave" or "David" for almost two years; a play on my last name of "Davies.")

I knew exactly what the question meant. As if he didn't already have enough on his plate, he was trying to brainstorm *other* things he could do to become even more successful. Trevor's brain just works this way. While I have to force myself to come up with ideas, his mind is automatically and constantly searching for new ones.

The question made me nervous. He expected me to already have ideas crafted to throw out at him, but I had none. Even if I started brainstorming on the spot, I wouldn't have one for a long while. He *did* want an answer. *What else can we do?* While I was content to enjoy the precarious situation we were in; living out of a van at a campground in Illinois for a week; Trevor felt like he was wasting time.

When I finally responded with, "I don't know. What kind of things are you thinking about?" I got an eye roll. My response wasn't an answer, but I hoped it would fuel some collaboration. If I could get Trevor to spill some of his ideas, I could begin to build onto them. That was better than offering up nothing. He took the bait and we launched ourselves into an all-night-long conversation. We talked about the things that made us tick. We discussed our feelings about more "normal" lives than the ones we were living. We talked about where we could be in life versus where we were.

At first, the conversation made me uneasy. It was circling all around a topic that I dreaded. Since the trip had started, I began to feel like I wasn't doing anything important or worthwhile enough with my life. Trevor, on the other hand, knew what he was working so hard for. He had a master plan and everything he was doing went back to that plan. I was pushing myself just as hard, and certainly harder than I ever had, but for what? I didn't have a master plan. I wasn't sure what my life was supposed to focus around. Was he disappointed in that?

Slowly and carefully, I tried to describe this feeling that I had been dragging around to Trevor. Racing and nutrition were his "things" and I described my worry about not having a "thing" of my own. As I did my best to explain, I searched Trevor's face for any sign of disappointment. He gave none. Instead, he provided me with a suggestion like he had known all along I was going to bring this topic up.

"Your *thing* is creativity." He said it like a fact, not an opinion. It made perfect sense, and yet I had never thought of it. Creativity has always been a driving force in my life, but I never considered it something I could become successful with. Yet, I always work ten times harder on a project when I get to be creative. I was still *creating* a successful business. It was creativity, along with a lot of determination and courage that had gotten me so far already. It could only take me higher from there; I just hadn't realized it.

The conversation continued on well past the late summertime sunset and deep into the night. We talked about ourselves; we talked about each other; and we talked about plans and dozens of ideas we had for the future. The conversation brought up topics most twenty-somethings never even consider. We joked that one day we would have to write a book about our unusual young lives. Maybe we could get someone to interview us about all of these ideas and philosophies and write the book for us. We certainly didn't have the time or know-how to do it on our own. Regardless, that would be light years away.

We fell into a routine for the next two days. We would have bananas for breakfast, and maybe some salted brown rice. Trevor would head off to ride the trails around the lake for a few hours while I stayed at the camp to work or took my camera out to explore. We would take turns showering at the spider-filled bathhouse at the campground and then grab our backpacks to ride to town. Each day we got as much work done as possible from the coffee shop with slow Wi-Fi. Then, we explored or tried to find faster Internet options before riding our bikes back to the campground.

When we got back from town on the third day, the campground was nearly full for the three-day, holiday weekend. The extremely low camping fees resulted in a campground full of very interesting folks who were planning on celebrating the 4th of July *much* harder than we were. We felt oddly out of place with our skinny cyclist legs and shirts that covered our bellies. While the apparent difference in lifestyle between us and our new campground neighbors made me uncomfortable at first, I looked past the differences and appreciated the fact that few people live their lives in the exact same ways. *Just like us, every person there that weekend had hopes and dreams of their own. They each were facing struggles and challenges that weren't apparent to us, but that they deal with every single day.* Even more, there wasn't a person there who didn't offer us a beer and invite us into their little "camp community" despite our apparent differences. It was a perfect way to celebrate being American and the important things we did have in common.

I sat at our campsite's splintery picnic table and tried to focus on getting some work done as firework sparks occasionally flew my way. Between the fireworks, blaring Led Zeppelin, and the never-ending influx of bugs, I was having a tough time being productive. I considered riding all the way back to town just to get out of the chaos, but what was the point? Instead, we chose to embrace it and raise a couple of cold ones into the air with our new, patriotic friends.

The day before the Macomb race, we woke up to the irritating buzz of flies as they circled our heads and tried to land on our noses. The bugs were out of control. Thankfully, it was our last full day in Macomb before the race and then our immediate departure the next morning. I was sick of the bugs, the noise, and ready to move on with the trip.

We took one last ride into town and decided to try out the Wi-Fi at McDonald's rather than endure the snail-paced setup at the old-fashioned coffee shop. We stepped into the McDonald's with our helmets still on, and found a corner where we could be out of the way with our bikes. Macomb just didn't seem like a safe place to leave bikes outside and expect them to not be stolen or harmed. One fierce kick from an undisciplined child to the carbon components on Trevor's bike and the entire thing would be out of commission. The bikes were coming inside with us and there was no discussion about it.

After ordering a drink, we propped the bikes up against the end of our corner booth, so they wouldn't be in the way of anyone in the nearly empty restaurant. I pulled out my laptop and smiled as one of the McDonald's employees walked past us. Except, she didn't smile back and she didn't walk past us.

As if I had just given her a dirty look rather than a smile, she spat out, "Your bikes belong outside, kids. You need to take them out *now*." She gave a look like she was both disgusted and furious with us. Her eyebrows were raised expectantly and her lips formed such a deep frown I wondered if she was even capable of smiling.

Leaving the bikes outside was just not an option. Instead, we were kicked out of McDonald's for the first and hopefully last time in our lives. I understood why they might not want bikes in the store, but I did not understand the need to be treated like vermin.

She would have scooped us into a dustpan and thrown us in the trash if she were able.

We headed further down the highway to the Burger King we visited a few nights prior. Not wanting to be kicked out of another fast food joint, we stashed ourselves discreetly in a corner table near the play area. Our bikes, at least, were not visible to the employees behind the counter. As lunchtime rolled around, the play area started to fill with the shrieks and squeals of happy children. Occasionally, it also filled with the awful wailing of a toddler who had bumped his head on some foam padding. Once we could no longer tolerate the jolting chorus of sounds, we packed our bags and rode back across the street to Wal-Mart to pick up groceries for the next couple of days.

Walking our bikes through the superstore brought a variety of reactions. Some people laughed at us while others stared with great curiosity, as if they'd never seen a set of wheels before. Every young child we passed loudly asked their mothers why we had bikes.

I couldn't help but think if we had done the same thing in a city like Boulder, the reaction would be different. Instead of getting looks that asked, "Are you even allowed to bring those mysterious contraptions inside?" we would be greeted with "Are those twenty-nine inch wheels or twenty-seven-point-fives?" We were truly in a whole new world.

Always Push Onward - Trevor

Anyone who has ever ridden a bicycle for an extended period of time can appreciate the luxury of padded bike shorts. This was one of the first lessons I learned when I traded a motor for pedals. Curiously, I continued to make the seven-mile trip into town from our interesting Macomb, Illinois campground/home in my beat up old cargo shorts. While the slightly downhill ride into town wasn't very bad, the journey back always left me awkwardly standing up and shifting my weight on my seat in discomfort.

I hadn't seen a single cyclist since crossing the border into Illinois. Every time I had been fully kitted up in my lycra, Audi race suit and riding to a trailhead, toothless gentlemen in large trucks had yelled an array of colorful comments to me regarding my sexuality.

Things were definitely different out here, and I wanted avoid sticking out too terribly much, especially while Sierra and I were vulnerably riding alongside the highway. Getting hot, sweaty, and extremely sore in street clothes while riding was a small price to pay if it meant fewer Slurpees being thrown at us (a terrible gesture angry motorists often extend to road cyclists) and interesting comments being yelled in our direction.

After our eventful afternoon in downtown Macomb, we just wanted to get back to our campground. We had posted up there in the heat, humidity, and ungodly mosquitoes for an entire week; all for the race that was now just a day away. We were both really looking forward to riding back to the van, whipping up another panfull of dinner, and then getting to bed. Unfortunately, the Macomb weather had different plans for us.

About half way back to our campground, the sky started to grumble as lightning flashes struck down in the distance. With bags of groceries hanging off our handlebars and filling up our backpacks, the last thing we were in the mood for was rain. More importantly, we had our computers and some filming equipment with us, which surely would not survive an Illinois rainstorm.

Our slow and dispirited cruise back to the van suddenly turned into an urban Tour de France. I started hammering down on the pedals, forgetting all about the pain from my stiff seat or the sack of potatoes bouncing off of my back, pounding into my kidneys.

Fully understanding the situation, Sierra hopped right on my wheel and into my draft. Looking equally as ridiculous with a huge bundle of bananas hanging from her handlebars, I paced her back into the campground at high speed. I could tell she was exhausted, struggling to hang on, and struggling with her bike seat just as much as I was. Still, the only thing worse than her physical state was her fear of getting her camera wet, which is what continued to fuel her pace.

We made it back to the van just as the sky really began to open up. The result was a rainstorm unlike anything we had ever seen before on the West Coast. Sheets of water fell from the sky and immediately flooded the grassy area around our campsite. Fortunately, we got our backpacks and electronics into the van just in time.

What had me most worried about the rain was how the van would hold up. Compared to this, the rain we had experienced in Montana was a minor trickle. Still, that little bit of water was enough to nearly burn the van down and almost end our entire journey. After that incident I had gotten some electrical tape and weather strips and made my best effort to fix the leaks. Was it successful? We would find out in the morning when I started the van to drive to the race.

In the mean time, we made our best attempt to seek refuge inside of the small bug-net canopy that we had purchased in an effort to protect ourselves from mosquitoes. We quickly realized that all of the mosquitoes, beetles, bees, flies, and spiders actually had the same idea and had beat us to this poor excuse for a shelter.

The van was unbearably hot from the humidity combined with baking in the sun that morning, so seeking shelter there was not even an option. Instead, we opted to accept the irony and share our bug tent with half of Macomb's insect population while getting soaked from the spray of endless rain plummeting down all around us. After about two hours of Googling, "Do hurricanes happen in Illinois?" the storm finally seemed to pass. We did our best to dry things out enough to make dinner and then we immediately headed to scope out the race venue, trying to beat the rapidly falling sun.

After the downpour, I knew it was possible that the race would be canceled. The idea didn't sit well with me after the amount of discomfort we had endured all week *just* for this event. Fortunately, the trails seemed completely rideable. I knew the race would be slippery and tough, but I was fine with that. I was assured even further that the race was still a "go" after running into an organizer who confirmed things were still on for the morning. *Awesome.*

We had made it right to the finale of our stay in Macomb, and I was anxious to get the race over with and get back to the Pro XCT series. I knew my odds of getting the win and earning points were high, as I was the highest ranked pro on the rider list. Just one last uncomfortably hot night in the van and we would be out of there.

Around 1 a.m. I heard it. The sound woke me from the deep sleep I had learned to achieve despite the rough conditions. What was the sound? Rain... *A lot* of rain, to be exact. It was coming down so hard you could not even hear the drops hitting the metal roof of the van anymore. Instead, the wall of water just sounded like the rumble of a subwoofer maintaining a steady bass level.

I tried to ignore it and fall back asleep. What good would stressing about it do? I figured the organizers *couldn't* cancel the race at this point. I had spoken with them just hours before and they assured me things were still on. The rain couldn't be so bad to make them change their mind on such short notice, right?

I tossed and turned all night long while the rain continued, relentlessly. My anxious mind ran through all of the different scenarios that might play out once the sun rose.

Best-case scenario, they still held the race. Though it would be a disgusting mud race that would probably ruin my jersey, shorts, helmet, and bike, at least I would get some valuable USA Cycling points for a better start position at Nationals in a few weeks.

Worst-case scenario, they would cancel the race. Maybe I'd get my entry fee back, but I definitely wouldn't get our campground fees back. Further, I wouldn't get back hours spent tossing and turning in the brutal Illinois heat and humidity while I should have been sleeping. Even more, I wouldn't get a single USA Cycling point.

While neither of my options were very good, I had my mind set on racing. Unfortunately, that wouldn't happen on this rainy weekend in Illinois, as I heard my phone chime with an email notification around 6:00 a.m. *The race was canceled.*

I had barely slept at all and hadn't stopped sweating since we left Colorado. Still, as soon as I read the email from the race promoter, I felt myself fill with frustration as I squeaked my way off the damp, rubber air mattress. I *needed* those USA Cycling points and I couldn't believe all of our Illinois troubles had been for nothing.

Sierra could tell I was in a bad mood and she definitely understood my frustrations. In fact, she had plenty of her own. Since arriving in Illinois, she had become absolutely covered in mosquito bites, chigger bites, and was just beginning to break out in hives due to an unknown allergy that she was developing. Even though she wasn't the one racing, she wanted some kind of closure from Macomb, too. She wanted the unpleasant week to have been worth something. Sadly, it seemed as though it was all a waste.

My anger turned into focus as I tried to figure out the best way to handle the new situation. The next stop on our journey would be Racine, Wisconsin for some more filming. We weren't scheduled to arrive there until the following day, but the plan had now changed. Also, I now had to get a big workout in that day since I wasn't going to be getting the race intensity that I was planning on.

Sierra was wandering around our campsite as I ran through all of the options. I was so deep in thought it took me a while to notice her and how odd she was acting. It was as if she was looking for something in the grass, but we hadn't even been out in the grass since the rain started, so I had no idea what she could have lost.

"What are you doing?" I yelled to her over the sound of the rain, which had now slowed to a gentle sprinkle.

There was no response. She looked up at me just for a second with a look of disbelief on her face and then continued her mysterious search. I walked over to her and asked again, this time a little more concerned. Turns out, one of her muddy shoes she had left just outside the van that night had been stolen. While it's still a mystery, we believed the culprit was a raccoon, which we had quickly realized were quite vicious in this part of the country. Every night, we could hear these seemingly innocent animals fighting and screeching all throughout our campsite. I have no idea why they would want a shoe, but the 'coon tracks scattered around in the mud indicated these giant rodents were to blame.

Now, Sierra only had one shoe, adding a comedic twist to her already sad condition. It's safe to say she was done with Macomb and probably would not be coming back to visit any time soon. *While spirits may have been low, sometimes all you can do is cut your losses and make the most out of the new and unplanned situation.*

I discussed our options with Sierra, sitting under our bug-filled tent, with her one naked foot. While I still needed to train that day, we decided the best thing to do was to get out of Illinois and try to get out of the rain. Because we had awoken so early after receiving the bad news about the race, we would be able to make great time in getting to Racine. So we packed up our soggy campsite and got on the road.

As we started driving, the rain only got worse. I had the windshield wipers on maximum speed and then got a sudden sinking feeling when I remembered that I hadn't checked to see if my homemade door patches had been successful or not. While the door locks were now completely dead and no longer a threat, the power windows were still alive and well. If they got wet, a situation similar to that dreadful morning in Montana could occur.

When I realized this, the rain had gotten so bad there was a solid inch of water sitting stagnant on the highway. I had slowed to about thirty miles per hour to maintain control over the van in the dangerous conditions. There was no place to pull over to check my repairs, nor was it even remotely safe to attempt such a thing. All I could do was keep my eyes on the road and hope the van didn't go up in flames, like it had come so close to before.

Then, like a nightmare from the past, both of our phones began vibrating out of control while also making a terrible noise. It was another emergency weather alert. Sierra picked up her phone and calmly read the warning to herself. Though the panic was nowhere near what it was in Colorado the first time this had happened, I could tell it was serious by the expression on her face.

She calmly read aloud, "Tornado warning. Seek shelter now."

Without giving a response, I scanned the horizon for "shelter." Deep in rural Illinois, we couldn't just hop off at the next exit and get to work inside of a comfortable and safe Starbucks like we did in Colorado. Instead, we had no idea where the next exit even was. For all we knew, it could have been another twenty miles down the highway. Even if we found an exit soon, it was unlikely there would be any kind of shelter that we could seek refuge in.

One mile passed after another and there was still no exit to be found. With our eyes continuously scanning our surroundings for anything that resembled a funnel cloud, we nervously continued through the wall of water that was falling from the sky. Several gusts of wind grabbed the broad sides of the van, jerking the steering wheel under my white knuckles.

The nervous driving continued for a little over half an hour before we saw a sign for an exit ahead. Offering a slight feeling of relief, the wind and rain had begun to die down. Without any sign of civilization at the approaching exit, I decided to just stay on the highway and continue to get us farther away from the storm. It appeared as though we had already made it through the worst of it and stopping would have only provided time for the wind and rain to catch up.

After another thirty minutes of slow and cautious driving, it was safe to say we had escaped. Though it continued to sprinkle, the road was just barely wet and the wind had stopped completely. By the time we had reached the Wisconsin border, my nerves were only a distant memory. Now, I was fighting to keep my eyes open, a battle Sierra had lost shortly after the danger of the storm had passed. Fully understanding the risks of drowsy driving, especially in such unfamiliar terrain, I downloaded a free and cheesy audio book on my phone and put it on the van's stereo system.

As Sierra dreamt happily, probably of raccoons wearing shoes and the red flashing lights of GoPro remotes, I tried to wrap my mind around the shallow and dull plot of my new, free book. The author's voice was difficult to understand coming out of the blown out speakers inside of the van. I figured this was another unfortunate consequence of the internal door flooding that had happened back in Montana, but wasn't entirely sure. Still, the cheap entertainment provided enough stimulus to keep me awake and focused on the road.

Just as the main character was about to solve the very predictable "mystery" and apprehend the villain, I could faintly make out the Racine skyline in the distance. We had spent almost ten hours on the road and would arrive at our destination in the late afternoon.

A fairly small city on the shores of Lake Michigan, Racine reminded me a lot of an old, rusty sports car. Obviously, it had been loved deeply in the past, as huge buildings with stunning beauty and architecture lined the downtown area. The sunset lit up Lake Michigan in the background, creating an endless, glowing abyss of orange and red. The landscape was green and vibrant, even throughout the city. However, it was a ghost town. The majority of the large buildings that lined the main streets were vacant. Streets were cracked and worn, and the parking areas, seemingly built for a different era, were empty.

Still, Racine oozed with potential. The city had everything necessary to thrive again, like it seemingly had before. The only thing it needed was someone willing to accept the task of restoration and bring new life back to it. With some hard work and a little faith, Racine's best days are yet to come.

Since we had no time left in the day to get our course filmed, Sierra and I headed to the harbor to watch the sunset. Before completely unwinding, I did a quick yet intense TrainerRoad workout on my stationary trainer in the parking lot, just outside of the van. Repeatedly maxing out my heart rate at 200 beats per minute while pedaling on the trainer after driving all day was not something I particularly wanted to do. Nevertheless, my competitors were not going to be taking a day off just because I wasn't in the mood to train. With that in mind, I got to pedaling, going through the prescribed intervals for that day that Kyle had sent to me at the beginning of the week.

Drenched in sweat, I finished up my painful yet vital workout and toweled off in the back of the van. Once changed, I joined Sierra on the dock, overlooking the third largest Great Lake. We watched a few sailboats gently undulating in the water while the old-fashioned street lights turned on one by one behind us.

Once night was completely upon us, we strolled back to the van in the brisk, damp air. There was a Wal-Mart about fifteen minutes away where we would be sleeping that night. We were planning on getting up before the sun to begin prepping for the course we needed to film. If we stayed on schedule, we hoped to finish filming in Racine in about three hours, drive another three hours northwest to Madison, Wisconsin, then film a second course there. Two courses in two cities, all in the same day; we had our work cut out for us.

It would be tough, but knocking out both of the Wisconsin courses on the same day would greatly free up the rest of our week. It would also take a huge weight off our shoulders. This was especially important to me, since I had my third Pro XCT event taking place the following weekend in Portage, Wisconsin, just a few hours north of Madison.

Though my confidence had continued to grow after Montana and Colorado, the missed race in Macomb left me anxious. As ridiculous as it is, going fourteen days without racing is enough to make me worry about losing speed. With all of the traveling and not being able to really nail down a consistent training routine, my mind wasn't in the best place leading up to the race in Portage.

That night as Sierra and I set up our cramped bedroom inside of the van, we picked up the same deep conversation that we had shared in Macomb the week before. Specifically, we revisited the idea of writing a book. With the air mattress halfway inflated, we stopped what we were doing as the excitement of the idea took over.

I had been searching around on the web for several days now, exploring different "ghostwriting" services. This is essentially where an author interviews you regarding the topic you want to write a book on, then writes it for you. They don't get any of the credit for writing it, as your name is the one listed as the author on the final product. While this was appealing given our immense lack of spare time, it just wouldn't suffice.

I was completely willing to make the investment for such a service if it would adequately document the journey of a lifetime. Further, if our story could be accurately and passionately illustrated through words in a way that inspired others to step out of their own comfort zone even in the smallest way, it would be worth it.

The issue I found to be insurmountable regarding the idea of ghostwriting was the magnitude of this whole experience. Sure, we could find an author to write about our big road trip and some of the unique career endeavors Sierra and I were and still are working on. But what I was confident no ghost writer would be able to fully grasp was the essence and beautiful struggle that gave this life-altering journey its deeper meaning.

While Sierra and I are a lot of things, we are by no means authors. Still, we were the only ones that would be able to truly convey what this adventure was all about. Things like the excitement of a shower after going a week in the Midwest humidity without one; or the sheer terror of almost losing everything you own in a burning van aside the highway; or the uncertainty and humility of dedicating a life to something others deemed impossible or out of reach. This epic trip represented, on so many different levels, the change that we hoped to inspire in the world. The only way to share that was to articulate it ourselves.

The thrill of the conversation was too much for the hot, muggy van. As crazy as it sounds, even talking was enough to make us start sweating in the brutal heat and humidity. So we moved to the Wendy's in the parking lot just across the street from us. It was here, at a lonely corner table in an empty Wendy's, that we made one of the boldest and most naïve decisions of our lives – we were going to write a book. Just like the big drop on the Missoula racecourse, I didn't want to think about it too much. I *knew* it would pay off in the end. We just needed to go for it.

Until getting kicked out of the air-conditioned fast food restaurant sometime around 1 a.m. we sat and brainstormed. After crafting a rough outline, we went back to the van that night with a brand new excitement for the trip, life, and the idea of inspiring a generation to find their purpose in this world and unremittingly pursue it.

Our 4:30 a.m. iPhone alarms came way too quickly the next morning. Only sleeping for a handful of hours was tough, but excitement from the night before still lingered in the air. Further, the humidity and heat only seemed to have gotten worse, making the option of sleep seem only slightly more enticing than getting on the road and getting some of the warm, stagnant air flowing.

The start of the course we were filming was about ten minutes away, at a huge beach on Lake Michigan. I began running all of the cables from the power inverter, out the windows, and then taping them down. While I did this, Sierra mounted and tested each of the cameras before she linked them to their remotes. We were getting really good and really fast with our setup.

Just as I placed the last piece of tape to the final cable on the side of the van, the most incredible and vivid sunrise I have ever seen started to take shape behind me over the lake. As if she read my mind, I saw Sierra grab her camera and start walking towards the water.

We had an insane filming and travel schedule planned for the day, yet the beauty before us was both mesmerizing and paralyzing. At the risk of sounding cheesy or cliché, there was something magical about those few moments we spent admiring one of the simplest gifts Mother Nature gives to us every single day. For several minutes, absolutely nothing mattered as we took it all in.

Still stunned and thankful, we got back into the van and put our "game faces" on as the vibrant fire in the sky slowly went out. I heard the rhythmic beeps of each GoPro, one by one, as they sprung to life via Sierra's remote commands. Next, I heard the lower pitch beeps of the GPS units turning on and we were underway.

Sierra was getting pretty good at the overabundance of duties she had in the backseat of the van while we filmed. I was extremely thankful for this, because navigating these unfamiliar cities was not easy. Maintaining thirty miles per hour while angry and unpredictable motorists flew by required every ounce of my attention. Fortunately, traffic was light this early in the morning, and Sierra had the directions down to a tee.

The course was almost sixty miles in length and featured a few sections of road that we doubled back on. One of these sections was a huge freeway that I knew would be a nightmare once Racine residents began their morning commutes.

The first run through this section went fairly smooth. However, the second run was almost an hour later and traffic was picking up quickly. When we got back onto it, I felt my grip strengthen on the steering wheel as I hugged the shoulder of the road as tightly as possible, trying my best to not block the speeding motorists. Still, rushed drivers flew past us, sometimes just inches from the side of the van.

Fortunately, the section was only about two miles long. After a few minutes of very tense driving, I could see the small farm road ahead where Sierra said I needed to turn on. Still hugging the shoulder in dense traffic, I was about a thousand feet away from the turn when Sierra informed me it was a *left*, not a *right*, like I was planning on. This meant I had to somehow cross both of the packed lanes of traffic, with cars traveling upwards of seventy miles per hour, while I maintained thirty. Plus, I had to do it in a thousand feet and closing.

My heart rate shot up and my grip went immediately back to white-knuckle on the wheel. *This was going to get dicey.*

Trying to find an opening in the constant flow of speeding cars, I slowed to a stop on the shoulder. After nervously waiting for what felt like an eternity, I saw a tiny gap. I told Sierra to hold on and gunned it.

Probably breaking some kind of world record for speed in a van, we narrowly made it to the turn lane on the left side of the road. Suddenly, the light at the intersection turned red, and I slammed on the brakes, causing the majority of our tightly packed belongings to slide out of their homes and towards the front seats. It wasn't pretty, but we made it.

The intersections were confusing in Wisconsin because they didn't have the white lines that show you where you are supposed to stop. Further, even in turning lanes, the arrows on the lights always point straight rather than left or right.

Having forgot about this in the chaos of just crossing the highway and getting to the turn lane, the light turned green and I continued just as the forward-pointing arrow on the light told me to. I crossed straight through the intersection and into a narrow, single-lane concrete shoot, assuming it was a special turn lane. Once I reached the end of it, I was back on the two lane, chaotic freeway. Only this time, I was headed *in the wrong direction.*

Once I wrapped my brain around what had just happened my heart sank. I had just re-entered this gnarly freeway on the other side, going the wrong way. I had been worried for our safety moments before while heading down this road in the correct direction, and now we were illegally traveling backwards on it.

In what was surely a miracle, there was a small gap in oncoming traffic as I unknowingly entered this horrible road in the wrong direction. Once the potentially lethal error registered in my mind, I went for another van world record and yanked on the steering wheel like you would see in an overly dramatic action movie. Going from shoulder to shoulder on this horrific two-lane highway, I somehow managed to whip the van around in a split second, narrowly escaping the stampede of oncoming traffic. The violent maneuver nearly yanked Sierra out of her seatbelt in the back seat and sent our already displaced belongings slamming into the passenger-side wall of the van. Things had gotten sketchier than I would have liked, but we were alive.

We were quickly back onto peaceful country roads but I couldn't stop my hands from shaking for the remainder of the course. I wanted to call it a day right then and there, but I knew time was of the essence.

Thankfully, the rest of the filming in Racine went off without a hitch. Despite the utter chaos that had taken place, we were still right on schedule for the day. *Next stop: Madison.*

The peaceful three-hour jaunt to Madison helped me calm down and regain my composure before the next course. Madison is an incredible university town with lush, green trees and bright blue bodies of water everywhere you look. However, the Wisconsin capital was also much bigger than Racine, and much more populated. This, combined with the time of day, meant we were sure to be facing significantly more traffic. I wasn't thrilled with this challenge, but I was accepting of it.

Unable to find anywhere to park my awkwardly large van, I illegally parked under a large bridge so that we could begin setting up (curious why we haven't gotten any parking tickets yet? Us too.) There was very little conversation between Sierra and me as we set up the cameras and prepped the van. We were both tired, focused, and ready to get the job done.

Madison had way more traffic than Racine, but the speed limits were much slower. This made it a lot less stressful due to fewer cars trying to pass us. As we got out into the countryside, the mood began to lighten as we took a few deep breaths and admired the scenery in the heart of America's Dairyland. The rest of the sixty-mile course seemed to fly by smoothly and almost effortlessly.

Obviously exhausted, we cruised to the finish, tore down the cameras, and headed towards Portage. Before leaving Madison, I stopped at a gas station on the outskirts of town to fill up. While the fuel was pumping, I walked around the van, inspecting it for any potential issues. My inspection was cut short as I made eye contact with Sierra through the side window and noticed she was on the verge of tears. Suddenly uninterested in anything else, I opened to door to see what was the matter.

"I think I need to go to the hospital. Or urgent care. Or somewhere!" she told me, visibly distraught.

Completely alarmed and confused, I asked her what was wrong. She had been complaining about what she thought was a sequence of bug bites around a *particularly* sensitive location below the belt on her body. She had become more and more vocal about the situation all day, but I didn't think much of it. After all, I was covered in bites, too.

That morning her condition had worsened, to the point where she was having a difficult time walking around or sitting due to the discomfort. It no longer seemed like bug bites were to blame. While I should have been more concerned, she did an incredible job of fighting through the pain while we took care of business that day on our two courses. So much so, by the time we had finished in Madison I had almost forgotten entirely about it.

Once the work was finished for the day, she couldn't hold it in anymore. It seemed as though the issue was not related to insects at all. Rather, it appeared as though she had discovered the East's version of poison oak – poison ivy. *And it was bad.*

Be Tough - Sierra

All I could think was, "*Give me a tranquilizer. Take me to the hospital. Somebody please put me to sleep.*" The itchiness. The pain. It consumed my every thought. Even sleeping didn't chase away the discomfort. I hadn't slept more than a couple hours the past two nights. I wanted somebody to just knock me out. For the past two days, everything I did or didn't do was dictated by the agony between my legs. It hurt to sit, but it hurt even worse to stand. Walking was nearly a cause for me to pass out. Simply moving my legs at all caused my eyes to well up with tears.

Every time I had to get out of the van to go into a store or sit down at a Starbucks, I tried to recall places I might have encountered the poison ivy. Unfortunately, the answer was fairly clear and extremely embarrassing to admit.

During our stay at the campground in Macomb, we had been using the wilderness to take care of business when it was too inconvenient to walk the half-mile to the restrooms. At night, without flashlights, it was often just easier to sneak into the bushes. I had never done this before, but one of the nights it seemed like a good idea to wipe after peeing in woods. You know, just to be extra clean and dry. What could it hurt? Clearly, I had grabbed the wrong kind of leaf, and now I was suffering greatly for it. (It's okay. You can laugh.)

Filming in Wisconsin had been torture. It took all of the energy I had to focus my mind on anything but my suffering. I had to watch the blinking red remote lights, our speed on the GPS devices, and most importantly, the course map. Every time we reached a stop sign, I rocked forward with the momentum of the van and my body tensed in agony. Instead of acknowledging it, I had to keep my eyes from tearing up so that I could watch and record the time of the stop.

It wasn't until we finished filming that I realized the task had actually been helpful in forgetting the poison ivy I was sure I had. As difficult as it had been to carry out all of my filming jobs, it had kept a part of my brain busy. When filming was finally done for the day, I now had nothing to distract me.

At that gas station, I practically begged Trevor to take me to a hospital. I wasn't sure what they could do for me, but I was afraid of my quickly worsening condition. As I tried to search for a hospital nearby in Madison, Trevor remembered something. He had had poison oak all over his arms and face earlier in the spring from a race in California. He had gone to see the father of one of the kids that he coached, who just happened to be a physician that specialized in treating allergies. With some creams and a prescription to ease the itch, Trevor's poison oak cleared up in just a few days.

Before heading to a hospital, we decided to call our physician friend back in Reno to see what he thought we should do. Trevor told him (through a few giggles) about my situation. Based on our knowledge of poison oak and the direness of the situation, he could confirm over the phone that I most likely had poison ivy between my legs. He prescribed me a generic prednisone prescription and sent it to a nearby Wal-Mart for us to pickup. After the two longest days of my life, an end was finally in sight.

I made the long and painful journey through the parking lot and into the store, only to find that my prescription was still a half hour away from being filled. I gimped around the store with Trevor as he picked up food for the night and next morning. I was waddling as if one of my legs was far longer than the other, but I didn't care. It was the only thing I could do to stay on my feet for more than a few seconds.

When I got the prescription pills, I swallowed them down as if they were the most delicious meal I had ever consumed. I only wished that they were of the instant-relief variety. Still, it helped to know that I might finally get some sleep later that night.

We drove two hours from Madison towards the town we would stay in until the next Pro XCT race that weekend. We headed for a campground at Devil's Lake State Park because we had heard there was some great riding there. We pulled into the State Park at dusk that same evening. Golden light shone in bits and pieces through overhanging tree limbs. The trees on either side of the winding entrance road made a surreal fairytale-like tunnel that I couldn't get enough of. For a few moments, the pain and itching was forgotten.

We wound our way through a maze of skinny, one-lane roads before locating the campsite that would be our home for the next three nights and days. Just as I had hoped, I made it through the night with a few more hours of sleep than I had been awarded in the two nights prior.

When I awoke in the morning, it wasn't to the rumble of vehicles in a Wal-Mart parking lot or to the sound of screeching children like we had in Macomb. It was to the sound of birds chirping melodic tunes instead. Even better, I slowly moved my legs and didn't experience the familiar lurching of my body as it responded to the discomfort.

After a hearty breakfast of rice and eggs, Trevor took off for a long ride. I needed Wi-Fi to get some work done which meant I had to travel at least a mile back to the park's main office. I wasn't sure if they even had Wi-Fi, but it was worth a shot.

The main office of the park resembled a small resort. There were several small food vendors outside and a large kitchen inside with twenty or more tables. It was a weekday and the place was nearly empty, so I brought my bike inside with me and chose a table with a window overlooking the lake below. I hadn't had Wi-Fi that fast or an "office" setting so quiet in over a week, so I became extra productive for a few hours.

I knew now that I had to take advantage of Internet wherever I could get it. With the long days of travel between busy race weekends, we never had much spare time to sit and work. Or, when we did have time, it was in the evening when we were already parked for the night, far away from any potential Wi-Fi sources.

I went back to camp eager to propose the idea of another video to Trevor, recapping the trip thus far. When he got back from his ride, though, he had other plans. I told him about the idea for the video, and he promised we could get to it in a few days. We didn't have time to dive into it that night because he had deemed it "book writing night."

We had talked about writing a book, made the decision to write it ourselves, and then even wrote an outline for it. After that, we'd spent a few days just saying we needed to start writing. We could talk about it and plan it all we wanted, but the book wasn't going to have any pages unless we started putting fingers to keyboards. As we sat inside the van and away from the bugs with our computers on our laps, our book began to gain its first of many pages.

I was twenty years old and writing a book. It sounded crazy, but it didn't feel crazy. Years ago, it would have felt crazy, too. But I had already accomplished so much, especially with Blü World Inspired, that writing a book became just another project with another set of tasks associated with it. Of course, the list of tasks was longer than any I had ever created before, but it didn't seem impossible. As soon as the book began, I saw a long, but clear path to its end.

I felt like I *should* have been overwhelmed by the entire concept. It should have felt impossible, and it should have made me want to pull my hair out. Rather, I was thrilled about it. It wasn't going to be easy, but it was going to be one of the most worthwhile things I could do with my young life. The book was going to challenge me in ways that nothing else could. Wasn't that exactly what I had wanted out of the trip? I wanted to step so far out of my comfort zone that I no longer needed to have a comfort zone. Most importantly, I would get to challenge myself by being the one thing that I always have been and always will be – creative.

After spending two nights at the expensive state park and enjoying running water and showers, we headed into the town of Portage to live like vagabonds in the town's Wal-Mart parking lot for a few days. We would have liked to, but we couldn't afford to stay at Devil's Lake any longer due to the high camping costs.

Staying in Portage was a nice change of pace after spending a week in Macomb. It was still small, but it felt refreshing and alive, whereas Macomb seemed dilapidated and dead. Our first order of business was, as almost always, to find Wi-Fi. We were lucky to find one coffee shop in the entire town. Coincidentally enough, we wandered into the small Main Street shop only a day after its grand opening. Had we been in Portage a day earlier, we would have been shocked to discover that fresh coffee was not at all available.

Behind the counter, a young man was still mulling over what prices to charge and what items to stock in his deli counter. It sounded like we were the first customers to order coffee that weren't family of the business owners. The shop had done a poor job of announcing its grand opening, as there wasn't even a sign out front.

While we sat at a small table and worked on our book, people wandered in from the street curious to see what kind of business was inside. Every person who walked into the brand new coffee shop walked out with a smile but no coffee. We felt for the new shop. The man behind the counter was clearly jazzed about his new life as an entrepreneur, and he remained upbeat as strangers walked in and back out without leaving their money.

Trevor ordered a second coffee before we left. I don't think he did it because it was good coffee or because he really wanted more. He did it because he had a soft spot for this struggling startup. We both wanted to see it succeed, because we knew how much effort the owners had put in to making their dream come to life.

Unfortunately, "The Percolator" hadn't set up public Wi-Fi, so we only stayed as long as we could manage to work on our new book, which ended up being a couple hours. Then, as writer's block consumed us both, we decided to start the Internet search once again. We spent the remainder of that day and the majority of the next seeking shelter from sporadic rainstorms inside the Portage public library. The library had also turned out to be the perfect place to work. The Internet connection was fast, the atmosphere was calm, and I swear the smell of old books made me work more efficiently.

The night before the race, we stayed in a very large, very expensive campground close to the race location. It was the only campground around, so we joined probably a hundred amateur racers in the campground while the rest of the pros slept comfortably in hotel rooms elsewhere. We had no choice but to fork out the extra dollars for the campsite. We needed to cook a real meal and showers were certainly in order.

When morning came, I began automatically preparing Trevor for race day. This was the fourth race of the trip, and I had the race day agenda ingrained in my mind. Trevor needed all three of his water bottles filled, each with a quarter scoop of electrolyte powder. One bottle was for him, and the other two were for me to give to him from the feed zone. I held his bike steady while he checked tires and lubed his chain. I handed him three zip ties, one at a time, as he put his number plate on. Then, I carefully but quickly safety pinned another number tag to his back, being careful not to cover up the pockets on his jersey.

Trevor, in his deeply focused state, didn't say anything as he rode off to warm up. I would see him at the starting line to top off his water if he wanted it and to grab anything from him that he decided he didn't need.

At the starting line, he needed neither water nor for me to take anything from him. I wished him luck and told him to "Kill it out there," just like I always do before a race. And, just like Trevor always does before a race, he said nothing back. He was so deeply engaged in his own mind, I never knew if he even heard me at the start line.

I headed up the course to stake my position in the feed zone, the area designated for water bottle exchanges. Local races didn't have such a section, but these Pro XCT's were highly structured and formal. At least one person for each of the nearly one hundred riders was crammed into a tiny strip of grass alongside the course. All of us had waters for our riders, and most had various other objects like spare sets of wheels, tools, and coolers full of ice. Trevor and I didn't have the luxury of bringing along such extras.

I heard the announcer count down the race start, and I waited a few seconds before the leaders came by in a *whoosh* of tires on grass. Trevor had to start at the very back of the pack again, despite having earned points in Montana and Colorado Springs that should have bumped him up. For one reason or another, this race was lined up by registration time, rather than points. With the van acting up, we never knew if we were going to make it to a race or not. Thus, Trevor had waited to register for the Wisconsin event the day before the race. Only one other person had registered after him, and the two of them were punished for it by being placed in the very last row of the pack. It was the last thing we had expected or wanted. I was more nervous for Trevor than I usually was during his races. The course was so twisty and turn-y, there wouldn't be many places to pass. Would he make up enough ground to have a decent finish?

Each lap took about sixteen minutes, but it felt like an eternity. I busied myself with checking and double checking the two water bottles I held, making sure that I had, in fact, remembered to add the electrolyte powder to them. As soon as the leaders came by, I began counting. It didn't matter what place Trevor was in each lap, but I liked to know. Plus, it kept me busy. *Eleven – Twelve – Thirteen.*

He probably didn't want to take a water bottle from my outstretched hand for the first couple of laps, but I dutifully held one out for him as he sped by me in the feed zone anyways.

As the third lap began, so did the rain. The race started out as a mountain bike race, but the freshly created mud turned the race into a slip-and-slide competition. As the riders passed by the feed zone going onto their fourth lap, they were covered in mud. Some had mud skid marks from their shoulders to their ankles. Those who hadn't crashed in the slippery conditions still battled them fiercely. I watched as riders took water bottles from their feed zone partners and used them to rinse their bike chain rather than to drink.

I saw Trevor approaching and I hoped he would take the water to clean his bike, but instead, he blew right by me again. His bike was caked with mud, and I was worried he might not be able to finish two more laps unless he did something about it. At this rate, I just wanted him to finish.

The rain continued to come down for the last half hour of the race. Apparently, rain in the Midwest is common enough that spectators all came prepared with umbrellas and rain jackets. I was the only one in the feed zone who had neither. My thin cotton sweater didn't even have a hood.

I watched Trevor go by the feed zone one last time, finally taking a water bottle from me. Based on the places I was counting each lap, he had made up a considerable amount of time during the rainstorm.

Soaking wet, I jogged across the small mountain to the finish line and watched as Trevor came through only a few places outside of the money-paying range. He had done so well, especially considering his dead-last starting position. Better yet, the finish was his best of the trip thus far, and he accumulated a lot of points that would help him with a better start position at National Championships the next week in Pennsylvania. He still had a ways to go to be in first place, but it felt like we were on a winning streak.

I held Trevor's bike for him as he hosed it off at the bike wash station immediately after the race. I was already soaked from the rain, so I didn't mind when he accidentally sprayed my legs, my arms, and sometimes my face. With the humidity, I would likely never dry off anyways. Trevor was the only person washing a bike in his racing kit, because all of the other pros had a pit crew to take care of the job for them while they got to relax.

We didn't have the luxury of having bikes washed for us, and we certainly didn't have the luxury of relaxation. As soon as I finished drying Trevor's bike, we got right back on the road. Our hectic schedule officially started back up. It was Saturday, and we had until Thursday *at the latest* to film a course in Indiana and then make it to Nationals in Eastern Pennsylvania. In our usual, chaotic fashion, we packed up Trevor's race bike, changed into dry clothes, and jumped on the freeway towards Chicago.

Part 5 – The Peak of Summer

Remember How Far You've Come - Sierra

I looked over at Trevor as we got on the freeway after leaving the race in Portage and noticed that he hadn't even wiped the mud from his face and arms. The small brown spots made his skin look something like a robin's egg, if the eggs were tan instead of blue.

We were headed for Pennsylvania, with mountain Bike Nationals now only a week away. Though the last two races on our tour, the World Cups, would be the largest and most challenging, Nationals was the most important. It was Trevor's best chance at getting atop the podium and would attract the most attention from potential future sponsors. We had to get there as soon as possible to be fully prepared for the most vital weekend of our trip.

The drive south and east brought us back to Madison, where we decided to stop and eat. After such a great race result that day, we decided to splurge and use the Olive Garden gift card we had brought on the trip with us. The gift card had been a birthday present for Trevor months ago, but we were saving it for a special occasion. After being on the road for nearly two months, it felt like a worthy time to spend it.

We were seated in a large booth in the corner of the restaurant, probably kept out of the open areas because of how haggard we looked. Not wanting to waste any time, we ordered immediately. Olive Garden only has two entrées that are gluten free anyways, and we know both of them by heart. Trevor got the only gluten free pasta dish that the restaurant offers and I ordered my all-time favorite endless soup.

Trevor was falling asleep at the table as he ate, his face still sprinkled with dirt. I hoped our waiter, who dutifully came to check on us every few minutes didn't notice how badly we needed to shower.

Our waiter was so on point. Any time we ran out of salad or I ran out of soup, he was instantly rushing another to our table. It wasn't because he had nothing else to do. We were eating during prime dinner time on a Saturday evening and the place was packed. The restaurant was chaotically busy. Still, Jeff, our waiter, never missed a beat and was happy to engage in small talk with us as well, despite the ten or so other tables he was tending to.

I've had good waiters and waitresses before; ones who never bring the wrong food and who always have a forced smile plastered across their face, but I had never seen a waiter like Jeff. Unfortunately, people who work *that* hard are not that common. It's one thing to be able to do your job properly, but to do your job, exceed your job's expectations, and do it without becoming stressed or overwhelmed is something else entirely.

These people with incredible talents or amazing work ethic often get blended into society wherever they can find a place because no one has told them that they are capable of more. With that kind of ability to work so hard at something, our waiter could go out and do just about anything he wanted, and likely succeed at it. Who knows, maybe he was in the process of doing that or maybe he loved his job and didn't want anything else. But his potential was endless. Not everyone has that kind of hard-working drive, but those who do can't be stopped once they realize it. *Work ethic is an invaluable characteristic that will eventually determine any entrepreneur's potential.*

After the delightful dinner splurge, we continued our journey south towards Chicago. We had another evening of driving past midnight to complete. Not long after we crossed the southern border of Wisconsin and headed into Illinois again, the rain began coming down. *Did it ever stop raining here?* The further south we drove, the harder and heavier the rain fell.

Our phones began the dreadful alarm sound that we were now accustomed to. This time, it was a flash flood rather than a tornado warning, which sounded slightly less frightening. At first, we didn't pay much attention since it wasn't advising us to take shelter. But then, the map on Trevor's phone began to fill up with small red icons that indicated vehicle crash sites on the freeway ahead of us. If the map was correct, there were about a dozen accidents in the next twenty miles of freeway.

The raindrops that were coming down were too big to even be called "drops." The van's windshield wipers were struggling to remove the water fast enough. With low visibility, an inch of water already on the road, and numerous accidents ahead, we decided to pull off the freeway.

We took the first exit we saw, then found a large gas station and parked under its protective canopy. We filled our water bottles inside the convenience store and stretched our legs before going back to the van to wait out the storm. It was still early in the night by our travel standards, so we were going to get back on the road once it looked less dangerous.

While we waited at the gas station in the pouring rain for at least a half hour, I began to fall asleep in my seat. With the storm showing no signs of letting up, we were forced to modify our travel plans even though we had wanted to cover more ground that night. We searched for a Wal-Mart nearby that we could sleep at, but there wasn't one. The only other places we knew we were allowed to sleep at were truck stops and there happened to be one just across the street from the gas station we were at. We moved the van from under the canopy that protects the fuel pumps, across the street, and out into the rain where at least fifty semis were already parked for the night. Not wanting to be run over by any incoming big rigs, we parked as out-of-the-way as possible. As soon as the air mattress was full, Trevor immediately fell asleep, glad for the early bedtime. I enjoyed the thunderous pounding of rain on the roof of the van before eventually drifting off as well.

When we awoke at the truck stop an hour north of Chicago, we were far behind schedule. We needed to film in Muncie, Indiana that day, and we still had a five-hour drive to get there. As we approached Chicago on what felt like a ten lane freeway, I marveled at the giant city. The skyline was a picturesque silhouette from several miles away, until it became a wall of concrete and glass buildings crowding the sky above us. When we got nearer to the impossibly tall skyscrapers, I could no longer see where they ended hundreds of feet above.

Once in Chicago, we began to see signs for toll roads. Not wanting to pay, we instructed our Google Map phone app to avoid any routes that would charge us. Why pay to drive on one road when another is free? After a few minutes of driving past the city, we began our journey to Indiana on toll-free roads. Since most of the roads in the West are toll-free, we expected to take some slightly longer, scenic freeways that were barely any less convenient than the toll-route. What we actually encountered was a jumble of county roads, each one lasting only a few miles before we had to turn down the next. We were never heading in the same direction for long and the pothole-filled roads ensured we never drove faster than forty miles per hour.

After Trevor had listened to a free audiobook a few nights prior while I slept in the passenger seat, oblivious, he suggested we try listening to another to pass the time. We found a free novel by the same author and quickly became engulfed in the cheesy, but suspenseful plot. It wasn't much, but it was enough to help pass the time while we drove at forty miles per hour.

We arrived in Muncie in the middle of the afternoon, which normally wasn't an ideal time for filming due to the extra cars on the road. Nevertheless, we had to execute our plans regardless of the time of day in order to make it to Nationals on time. Traffic ended up not being an issue in Muncie, though. The small farm town was far enough out in the middle of nowhere that I wondered if cars ever drove on its roads. The course wasn't quite as long as the sixty-milers we had been filming, so we finished in just under two hours. Without giving Muncie any more of our time, we were back on our toll-free route to Mountain Bike Nationals in Pennsylvania.

As soon as the sun went down, I began the familiar struggle to stay awake. The audio book helped keep my mind from drifting for a while, but sleep finally came over me somewhere in Ohio.

Trevor really likes to scare me awake, so I try to never fall asleep while he is driving. Or, I try to fall asleep facing the window so he doesn't notice. This time, he spotted my closed eyelids and decided that I should experience West Virginia with him, even though there was nothing to see in the dark. He let out an abrupt, ear-drum-breaking shriek and smiled at me as I jolted awake. At first I was confused and then angry with him for letting out such an awful sound. But it worked – I was awake.

As we crossed rural West Virginia in the dark, faint mountains began to appear. For the first time in weeks, the road became something other than flat. I wished I could have seen it, but the sun had set on us hours before in Ohio where the roads are all level as a tortilla. After only an hour in West Virginia, we crossed the Pennsylvania border sometime well beyond midnight. Just after seeing the "Welcome to Pennsylvania" sign, sleep kidnapped my consciousness once again.

We must have stopped the van and Trevor must have blown up the air mattress because I woke up the next morning in a Wal-Mart parking lot and had no idea where we were. I hadn't remembered stopping anywhere or going to bed. Even though I wasn't exactly sure where in Pennsylvania we were, I knew one thing: we had made it to the East Coast. We had driven across the entire continent.

I never checked the map to see exactly where we stayed that night and I probably will never know. We took off immediately from the Wal-Mart and headed further east. Our toll-free route took us slightly south into Maryland before we continued back into Pennsylvania.

After driving for nearly two whole days, we were making great time towards Nationals. We arrived at the venue five days before

Trevor's race was scheduled. The winding countryside roads leading to the resort in Macungie, Pennsylvania, were such a nice change of pace from the farmlands we had become accustomed to. The last few miles before we arrived at the resort were so skinny that it would be dangerous to put your arm out your vehicle window. Old barns made from brick and large stone marked the edge of the road in some places, so closely that I worried about the side mirrors of the van being torn off.

The architecture of nearly every home and building we passed mesmerized me. I was taken back to a memory of the one house I loved most from my childhood hometown. It wasn't one of the many picturesque log cabin style homes, and it wasn't the giant mansion I affectionately called "Castle House." No, the house I loved growing up was a simple, ancient, two-story saltbox home. Something about the tall, perfectly rectangular brick home left me in awe.

In Pennsylvania, I saw nothing but saltbox homes. I pointed with excitement at each one we passed, until I resorted to quietly watching them go by. I could have deemed any one of them my dream home.

When we finally reached Bear Creek Resort, a ski resort in the wintertime and mountain bike metropolis in the summer, I was amazed at how large the event was. The resort building itself was a quarter mile long and very high class. On top of that, the grounds were already filled with people. Team tents already lined the venue and racers were coming and going on bikes in every direction.

Trevor picked up his rider packet and number plates from the registration table inside the resort while I read information about the race posted to the walls. Eager to ride the trails that wound up and across the lush ski mountain, Trevor kitted up and took off for a long pre-ride. He would be gone for a few hours, leaving me with a whole afternoon to explore the resort and mountain.

The weather was hot, but not nearly as humid as it had been in Illinois and Wisconsin, so I decided to try riding the amateur course. I had ridden a few laps of the amateur course in Montana and loved it. I had also ridden part of the course in Wisconsin before the swarms of mosquitoes became too much to handle and I cut my ride short.

I geared up and headed for the trails, already tired from the afternoon heat. The course started with a challenging rocky climb, punctuated by short, smooth sections. I've always been much better at going uphill than down, but this uphill became very frustrating very quickly. I was going so slow up the technical ascent that it would have been faster to just walk my bike. Every time I managed to successfully pedal up and over one large rock or root cluster, my front wheel ran right into the next large obstacle, stopping me dead in my tracks and forcing me to push my bike until the trail became tamer.

What's more, the lap was mostly uphill for the first two and a half miles, but short, frightening drops frequently disrupted the climb. Being a beginner of a mountain biker, I confronted most of these sections by clutching my handlebars as tightly as I could and hoping my bike chose the right line through the mishap of rocks and roots. Adrenaline filled my body every time as I nearly toppled forward over my handlebars. Sometimes I made it out clean, and other times I had to do damage control as I crashed haphazardly into the mud and rocks.

By the time I reached the crest of the mountain, I had been riding for nearly an hour. I should actually say I had been riding, crashing, and walking my bike over impossible rock obstacles for nearly an hour. I had the fitness to make it up the mountain, but my lack of technical skill meant the ride was mostly a struggle.

As I slowly made my way back down the mountain, I found myself having to walk often. I just couldn't see a way to successfully tackle the steep, rocky drops of doom. Even when I wasn't getting off my bike for impossible obstacles, I had to pull off the trail every other minute for a fast-approaching, more skilled rider. I could keep riding and make them get stuck behind me but the knowledge that someone might witness me crash down the next steep section was nerve-wracking. I was more than happy to let people go by so I could struggle in peace.

After nearly two hours, I was back at the bottom of the mountain and made the very easy choice not to go for another lap. When Trevor got back from his ride, it was the early evening, and we had to figure out where to make dinner. The organizers wanted to charge us thirty dollars per night to camp in a lot a mile away from the resort. The lot didn't have running water or a bathroom and we just didn't see the point of paying that kind of money when it would only inconvenience us. Instead, we opted to stay parked in the main lot, close to the resort and its amenities. We just hoped no one noticed when we spent the night there in our van.

We moved the van to the grassy outskirts of the main dirt parking area and set up our camp stove on the ground between two large pine trees that lined the lot. We had to remain as inconspicuous as possible because a few yellow-vested parking personnel were still wandering around.

Squatting on the ground in front of the camp stove, I cooked up a dinner of beef, gluten-free pasta, and vegetables. Still trying to be sneaky, we ate inside the van as the parking lot cleared out for the evening.

After dinner, we headed into the resort to find Internet and a comfortable place to work. We walked the entire length of the resort, passing meeting halls, restaurants, a ballroom, and a hotel all connected by corridors. At the very far end of the massive complex we found a tucked-away sunroom with two tables. Trevor and I claimed one of the large tables and began plugging all of our devices into the wall outlets to charge. We watched a colorful sunset form and then disappear through the large windows as we worked into the night.

For the next two days, our routine was nearly the same, except I decided against riding the course anymore. While Trevor rode, I spent more time behind my computer screen in the resort's sunroom, working on a few projects for clients as well as adding to our book. At dusk, we would sneakily make dinner between the same two large pine trees, trying to avoid parking lot patrollers.

A few people noticed us occupying the same table with our computers every day and asked what we were doing. Not in a prying way, but in an honestly curious way. When we told them our story, they could hardly believe that we had been traveling and racing while living out of a van for just about two months. When we said it aloud, we reminded ourselves of how crazy and shocking our journey must be to others.

After being on the road for so many weeks, the novelty of the whole trip had started to wear off. Surprises like finding out the van was too small to sleep in became fewer and fewer. It no longer seemed crazy to go three or four days without showering and crossing state lines had turned into a smaller celebration than when we had started. We had really begun to accept our VanLife; so saying it out loud was a reminder that we were doing something much larger than just traveling in a van.

On the day before Trevor's race, the first thing I did in the morning was seek out a shower. My hair was becoming a greasy disaster after I rode the course on the first day in Macungie. Trevor had been riding every day in the ninety-degree heat, and he was in need of one, too. I had high hopes for finding a shower in the luxurious resort, but after checking the bathrooms and locker rooms, I left disheartened. I had only one option left.

We packed a solar shower when we departed for our journey weeks prior. I had anticipated running into this exact issue and now

I was glad I had brought it. I wasn't sure where we would set it up, but I would figure that out after I filled it up and made sure it even worked.

The closest place to the parking lot that had water was a bike wash station, almost a quarter mile away from where the van was parked. The quarter mile walk there seemed short, but the quarter mile walk back with a forty-pound rubber sack of sloshing water was painfully long.

The large resort parking lot was completely full, so I received plenty of inquiring stares as I struggled to carry the awkward and heavy bag back to the van. To make it worse, the solar shower was so cheaply made its open/shut nozzle was not watertight. With every step I took, a dribble of water seeped out of the bag and down my torso. I tried carrying the bag like a baby, cradling it from under-neath. I tried to carry it tight to my chest like a stack of books with my arms crossed over the front of it. I even tried carrying it on my shoulder, the weight of the water awkwardly supported by the side of my head. By the time I got back to the van, my shirt was soaked and I had small streams of water dripping down my legs. The job must have been quite a sight for everyone who witnessed it. I hoped getting things set up then would save us time when we decided to rinse off after the race. Unfortunately, now I didn't even think there would be water left in the leaking bag by then. We would just have to wait and see.

By the day before Trevor's biggest race of the season, things were looking perfect. Though the weather had been hot, it wasn't miser-ably humid anymore. We had been able to sleep a full eight or nine hours each night, with no humidity or bugs to wake us from our slumber. We had even been eating fairly well. Plus, I was sure Trevor had ridden the course at least a dozen times, which meant he had his lines picked out through those tricky rock sections. Well, they probably weren't even tricky for him. To top it all off, there wasn't a drop of rain in the forecast for race day. Trevor couldn't have been more prepared for the biggest race of the summer.

Let Failure be a Motivator - Trevor

Due to the amount of time it takes to develop the legs, lungs, and heart necessary to compete at the top level of mountain biking, the professional level of the sport is broken up into two categories – one for pros that are under twenty-three years of age and one for everyone twenty-three and up.

While most places in the world put a ton of emphasis on the U23 (under twenty-three) division of pros, that's just not the case here in America. At every single race, including the Pro XCT events, all pros are thrown into the same field. While this makes it a lot more difficult for younger elite riders to stand out and make a name for themselves early on, it also helps tremendously in preparing young professionals for the "big leagues." Graduating from U23 is not a big deal in America, since nothing really changes at the domestic races.

The one exception to this are the USA National Championships. This is the sole event all year in the United States where young pros steal the spotlight in their very own race, separate from the older, more experienced elite riders. Winning a U23 National Championship is a very prestigious honor that any young fan of the sport has surely dreamt about at least once.

Originally, my goal going into Nationals was a solid top ten finish. This kind of result would be career altering, and it would remain on my resume for the rest of my days as a professional cyclist. After my race in Wisconsin the week before and my increasing Pro XCT success, I started believing that I was capable of an even better finish than just top ten.

Even before this summer, I had a good idea of who the strongest U23 riders in the country were. As racing got under way at the Pro XCT events, I was fairly surprised when I noticed I was finishing ahead of many of the highest ranked young professionals in the country. In Montana, I had placed ninth out of the other U23 riders, then seventh in Colorado, and finally fourth in Wisconsin. Knowing that, as well as knowing that I was headed to Pennsylvania with the best fitness and speed of my entire life, my goals changed. I knew that it would be a lofty task, but I set my sights on the podium.

The championship racecourse at Bear Creek Resort in Eastern Pennsylvania was extremely technical and rocky. It featured some steep climbs and even steeper descents as the three-mile loop wound across the ski slopes to the top of the mountain and back down. Though the weather had been clear and quite nice since leaving Wisconsin, a few of the sections on the course deep in the woods were still muddy. It was a textbook East Coast mountain bike course.

Before departing on this great adventure, a course like the one in Pennsylvania would have been a nightmare for me. Everything from the slippery rocks and roots that covered the face of the trails, to the thick and oxygen-rich air were the complete opposite of the trails I train on back home. Thankfully, I had been easing into this style of terrain all summer. The progression of the Pro XCT courses leading up to Nationals made for the perfect set of stepping-stones into the world of East Coast mountain bike racing.

When race day arrived, everything seemed to be coming together perfectly. My neck and spine seemed to ache less than usual from the cramped van sleeping. The temperature wasn't too hot or too cold. My bike was cleaned, tuned, and in great shape for the day ahead. There was just a feeling in the air that it was going to be a great day.

This feeling was only amplified when Sierra and I meandered into the lodge at the base of the ski resort. We were headed in to fill up water bottles at the drinking fountain and check our email before we turned our minds on to "race mode" for the rest of the day.

As I stood in front of the water fountain, slowly filling the first of many water bottles, my eye was caught by a piece of paper taped to the wall in front of me. The top of the paper read "Men's U23 Call-Ups." This list showed the order in which U23 riders would be called up to the start line.

Suddenly very interested, my eyes began scanning the piece of paper for my name. Due to my experiences at every Pro XCT before this race, I started from the bottom of the sheet and skimmed upwards. I expected to see my name, probably misspelled (electronic scoring systems really struggle with the accent in my last name), one or two places from the last rider on the list.

As I scanned up the sheet, each name that I read that wasn't mine began to fill me with a little more hope. By the time I reached the middle of the list, this hope began to fade as it was replaced with doubt. I had become so accustomed to last place start positions, I assumed there must have been an error and I was somehow left off the start list. Now deeply focused with growing nerves, I skeptically continued to scan upwards. *And then I saw it.*

I blinked several times and re-read the name to make sure it was mine. To my surprise, I was eighth on the list. This meant I would not be starting on the last row. Nor would I be starting on any of the middle rows, which I would have been more than satisfied with. This meant I would be starting on the *first* row of the fifty-rider field that contained the best young professional mountain bike racers in the United States. My strong finish in Wisconsin had given me enough points in the series to surpass all but seven other U23 riders in domestic ranking. It was a dream come true that only added to my high spirits and excitement to get the racing underway.

As I began warming up around the resort, I noticed a lot of familiar faces from the Pro XCT events that summer, as well as a lot of unfamiliar ones. Seeing so many new riders was a little nerve-racking since I had no idea what their capabilities atop a bicycle were. Still, I remained confident. I knew that the races I had already spent the majority of the summer battling in were the absolute pinnacle of North American mountain biking.

Excited and anxious for my front-row starting position, I was the first rider waiting in the staging area. I really didn't even know how this call-up process worked since I had never had the privilege of being apart of it, so I made sure I was there early so I didn't run the risk of missing anything important.

When the announcer got to my name on the call-up list, I heard, "From Reno, Nevada, riding for Audi/Specialized, Trevor De-Roose!" as I was waved to the start line. I hoped that if I could make this a regular thing, starting on the front row, maybe they would get my last name right in the future. But really, I was just happy to be there, on the front line of the most prestigious race in America.

As the masses of riders got organized behind me, there was a constant explosion of flash bulbs in front of us as reporters and photographers from all of the major cycling publications snapped shots of the field. The experience was almost overwhelming but it was everything I had imagined it would be.

I removed my helmet as the National Anthem started. An exceptionally talented young woman sang the timeless piece as the spectators who now lined the sides of the course from the resort to the top of the mountain fell silent. I almost forgot to breathe as the immense weight of the moment pressed down on me.

Immediately after the applause for the young woman, the announcer called out, "Thirty seconds until start!" *This was it.* The biggest moment of my young career was now upon me and the odds couldn't have been more in my favor. The hundreds of feelings and emotions that I had been filled with on the starting line were now gone. Everything fell silent as I gripped my handlebars firmly and double-checked my right foot to ensure it was securely locked into the pedal, as my left shook ever so slightly while planted on the gravel road below.

I took a deep breath and then the gun went off.

I hurled myself forward and stomped on the pedals with everything I had. The scratching sound of tires slipping on the gravel and the crunch of gears being forcefully shifted echoed off of the mountain, making the already substantial field seem even bigger.

I made a small error coming into the first turn leaving the gravel and heading out onto the grass of the ski slope. My front wheel slipped ever so slightly around the right turn, causing me to lose just a fraction of a second. The result was a wave of five riders immediately engulfing me.

Remembering my lessons learned from the early Pro XCT rounds, I reminded myself to stay calm and ride smart. This was going to be a long and tactical race. On top of that, the rock gardens would eat me alive if I didn't attack them perfectly each lap.

I remained content in my position for the entirety of the first lap. Nobody was really pulling away from our group, so I was happy to stay where I was and get some extra practice on the technical descents without having to push too hard.

On the second lap, I began moving forward. The tight and technical course was challenging to pass on, so I had to methodically pick my way around riders. Starting to really feel good, I grabbed a bottle from Sierra in the feed zone and headed out onto the third lap looking to start making a run for the front. There were only two laps left and no time to waste. My legs felt great, my bike was perfect, and my mind was definitely in the race.

I caught a group of three riders on the climb and was waiting for an opportunity to get around them as we picked our way through the rocks. We crested the top of the mountain and began back down towards the resort. Just as we hit one of the steepest and fastest parts of the descent, I saw a small opening and went for it. I jumped out of my seat and hammered on the pedals, quickly overtaking all three riders in an aggressive but calculated attack.

As I got back into the main line on the trail, my rear wheel caught a root and jumped out to the side. When it came back down to make contact with the ground, it caught a large rock. I could feel the torque and tension all through my carbon fiber frame as the bike tried to absorb the massive impact from the side. I tried to compensate for the shock by moving my body in the opposite direction. Instead, the bike whipped back, pointing straight down the trail for only a second before overcorrecting and shooting my rear wheel back out to the other side. This time, when it touched down I heard the dreaded sound of crunching carbon, as my state-of-the-art race wheel was smashed upon impact with the unforgiving Pennsylvania rocks.

Going about thirty miles per hour, I locked up the rear brake trying to salvage whatever was left of my obliterated wheel while also trying to save myself from slamming down onto the unforgiving, rocky ground.

Once to a safe speed, I felt slightly relieved that I was still in one piece. Relief quickly turned into despair as I examined my bike and knew my race was done. While I had the parts back at the van to repair it, my chances of a good finish at Nationals were long gone.

Utter devastation doesn't quite sum up my emotions as I walked my incapacitated bicycle down the ski slope back towards the resort. This was the single most important race of my young career. We had driven almost 8,000 miles already and spent almost two months on the road. For what? For me to blow it and break my bicycle?

These were the types of negative thoughts that filled my mind during my hike down the mountain. As I neared the resort and watched the leaders rip through onto their next lap, I wondered why that couldn't be me? Why couldn't I have just waited for a better chance to pass and played it safe?

Failure is a difficult thing to deal with on all levels. That day in Pennsylvania, I had failed tremendously. Both physical and mental consequences can often make one reconsider their goals and dreams. *However, failure is also the single most valuable learning tool known to man.*

I've spent a lot of time with some of the most talented and successful athletes in the world. Every single one of them will agree that the higher you climb, the harder you fall. While this sounds negative and pessimistic, I don't think it's meant to be. It's simply a truth that must be accepted in order to wholeheartedly chase a dream. If you can't accept it, then the first fall from whatever height you've made it to will almost undoubtedly be enough to make you reconsider the endeavor.

What a lot of people don't know about my life and myself is just how much and how hard I've failed in the past to get to where I am now. Since the age of four when I would make bicycle jumps in our backyard that were obviously way too big for my skill level at the time, I've understood this. I've understood that if you want to stand out, if you want to do something big, you have to be willing to fall flat on your face. Believe me, I gave my parents plenty of scares doing just that on my backyard bicycle park, and I've never stopped.

I feel the key to overcoming failure and hardship is to fully understand and accept it before even getting yourself into an endeavor. This way, you know for sure that your dream or vision is worth more to you than the potential downfalls that might come along the way. If you decide they are, you have to hold on to that. When you've been kicked to the ground and are thinking about giving up, look back to that moment when you decided that it was all worth it. Remember *why* you decided it was worth it. Remember the passion and spark you felt that made you courageously go after something, while understanding full well the risks involved. *This* is how you persevere.

As I made my way to the van, Sierra came running from the feed zone wondering why I hadn't come by for another lap. One look at my facial expression and she didn't even need to see my exploded wheel. She had seen that face before and she knew what it meant. While Sierra is the type of person I can tell anything to and get nothing but love, empathy, and compassion in return, I was in no mood to even say a word. Fortunately, she seemed to understand that.

With a simple "I'm so sorry," she unlocked the van and gave me my space. Before long, the emotions running through me were all overtaken by sheer determination and hunger. Yes, Nationals were a bust. I made the decision right then to do everything in my power to make the most out of the remaining races and still leave an impression on the North American mountain bike scene that summer.

My newly rebooted and anger-filled motivation was focused on the Super-D National Championship. This is a mostly downhill, sprint event that was taking place there at Bear Creek just a few days later. The course was gnarly, rocky, and fast. Having a bike designed for Super-D racing and riding was extremely important. These kinds of bikes were tougher, stronger, had lower seats for more maneuverability, and had advanced suspension for absorbing rocks and big hits at high speeds.

I didn't have this type of bike, so my cross-country machine would have to do. After getting the rear wheel fixed, I rode the Super-D course twice and then waited for race day.

As an ex-motocross racer, people constantly tell me that I should put more effort into racing these types of events. With the high speeds and need for immense bike handling skills, Super-D seemed right up my alley. I had raced one before back home in Nevada on a cross-country bike, and I won by a pretty substantial margin. Still, that was a local race, not the United States National Championships. I had no idea what to expect, but I was going to "hold it wide open," as we'd say at the moto track, and go for broke.

Still mad about how the cross-country race had gone, my attitude on Super-D race day certainly could have been misconstrued as arrogant. Rather, I was just immensely focused, motivated, and far from being over the failure from earlier that week.

Unlike cross-country, there isn't a mass start in Super-D. Instead, riders start the course one by one, with only thirty seconds in between them. Before racing commences, each rider is assigned a start time. I just so happened to be assigned the very first slot, allowing me to take to the course before anyone else.

While the majority of my competitors rode the chairlift to the top of the mountain where the race started, I channeled my anger into doing some extra climbing intervals on the road that led to the top before racing got underway that morning. I wasn't too concerned with fatiguing myself before the race because Super-D wasn't what I had come all this way for, and I needed to still get my training in before the remaining races we had on our schedule.

I made it to the top of the mountain, sweaty and breathing hard. My competitors looked at me strangely on my cross-country bike, wearing my lycra Audi race kit. The downhill racing crowd typically chose to wear loosely fitting riding attire, unlike what I had on. Uninterested in the funny looks and fingers being pointed, I rolled right through the crowd and up to the start gate. I was good and warm from the ride up and entirely fearless since there was absolutely no pressure or expectation, even from myself, for a cross-country rider to do well in this type of event on ill-fitted equipment.

Three. Two. One. Go. The starter raised the flag and my mind went blank as instinct kicked in, and I charged into the woods and into the first rock garden. Rather than worry about the potential of every single rock to slice my tire and end my race like I had done when the stakes were high during the cross-country event, I *dared* them to try and give me a flat. I charged into them harder than I had all week, filled with attitude and bitterness.

My run was going well at the halfway point. I knew my rigid cross country bike wouldn't allow me to go quite as fast as the rest of the *real* Super-D racers through some of the high-speed and extremely rough sections. With this in mind, I tried my best to reduce the damage as I went through them and then make up my time on the more technical, twisty sections. If there is one thing I can do well on a bike, it's turn.

As I made it through the final obstacles, I sprinted to the line just as my lungs and heart began to scream for mercy. I crossed the line with absolutely no idea how my time would stack up against the best in the country, but I knew I had given it my all. Sure, had I had the right bike I could have gained some significant time through a few sections, but I couldn't do anything about this, so stressing over it was silly. Instead, I headed straight for the resort and just waited for the results.

One by one, riders came down the mountain while the announcers broadcasted their times. Some were ten seconds behind me, while others were minutes behind. At first, I was surprised but then I was just anxious. It was clear my time was fast, and now I just had to wait and see exactly *how* fast.

With only four riders left to go, I still had the fastest time of the day and by a significant margin. Things were looking good for my very first national championship, but it was far too soon to jump to conclusions. Two more riders finished and I was still comfortably in the lead. Then, all of a sudden, one of the announcers gasped into the microphone. He explained that they had a rider on course who had just come through the first split and was right on pace with the fastest time of the day. My heart rate shot up as I stared intently towards the mountain, as if I would be able to see whether or not this rider was actually faster. After a few agonizing minutes, the mystery rider crossed the line and I anxiously waited for his result.

Two seconds. He had beaten my seemingly unbeatable time by two measly seconds. I started thinking about every little improvement I could have made to make those two seconds up. Still, it didn't matter. It was over. The final rider came through, significantly off my time, and I was now the silver medalist at the 2014 USA Super-D National Championships.

The emotions that came afterwards were mixed. Part of me was excited about this unforeseen accomplishment, while another part of me was just disinterested. Super-D wasn't what I had come all this way for. While the result was substantial, I just didn't feel like celebrating. Perhaps that would have been different if I was taking home the gold rather than silver, or perhaps not. I had worked so hard for every bit of my cross-country success and all of the effort and sacrifice is what made each small accomplishment feel so significant. With Super-D, I had literally just winged it, and it worked out.

After the awards ceremony, I talked with a lot of people about the near win at the event as well as back home in Nevada. Many were surprised and urged me to take a more serious approach to this style of racing. While I would agree that I could probably have a lot of success if I made more of an effort towards it, I knew cross-country would remain my primary focus. There was just something addictive about the challenge an XC race provided that I *had* to conquer. I had come so close and I surely was not going to give up now. I figured Super-D and this style of event would always be waiting for me after I reached my goals and established myself well enough in the cross-country world.

Back at the van with my silver medal, I took a quick and shameless solar shower in the big grass field we had been living in. The giant bag of lukewarm water that Sierra had worked so hard to acquire was now nearly empty as it lay deflated on the ground. Still, it was enough for us to rinse off with. Satisfied to have salvaged some kind of success at Nationals, I was still filled with that same focus and determination that overwhelmed me after the XC race. There was no time to celebrate the Super-D performance, nor was there any interest in doing so. We had to get back on the road.

Next stop was Williston, Vermont, for the final Pro XCT of the season, which was set to take place in just six days. I now narrowed my focus on this race with the same intensity I had towards the U23 event at Nationals earlier in the week. This was my final Pro XCT of the year, and I wanted to make sure I went out with a bang.

The week ahead was going to be long, though, as we had two courses in New York to film on the way up to Vermont. These would serve as our first real East Coast courses to film and both Sierra and I were a little nervous due to the immense traffic and unfamiliar territory on this side of the country. All the while, we had to get up to Vermont in a timely manner to pre-ride the course and prepare for the final Pro XCT of the year.

Don't Judge a Book by the Cover - Sierra

We left Pennsylvania in an uncomfortable silence. I was so proud of Trevor for his second place finish in the Super-D event, but he was clearly disappointed with his misfortune in the cross-country race. I couldn't blame him. There was nothing we could have done about the wheel, unless we had a huge team of people ready with spares along the course like most of the other pros did. Would that have made a difference? There was no way of knowing, but it still bothered me.

As we headed north towards New York and Vermont, the mountains started to get taller. Evergreens began to replace the bright green deciduous trees that covered Pennsylvania. After an hour of traveling northbound, we jumped on a freeway to head west for a short while.

That westbound freeway happened to be Interstate 80, the exact same freeway we had started our journey on back in Reno. Even though Interstate 80 spans the entire continent, being back on it felt surreal. I-80 sounded like a place reserved for "home" and yet we were so unbelievably far away. For a moment, the United States felt like a small, cozy little country rather then the immense expanse of land that it is. Driving across it makes it feel smaller – puts it all into a new kind of perspective.

If we stayed on I-80 and drove from Pennsylvania to Reno without stopping, we would be home in less than two days. That didn't sound that far at all. Crossing the New York border also helped solidify my feeling that the states really aren't so huge. New York was a place I had only heard stories about. It was the place of large buildings, angry drivers, and Niagara Falls. Though I knew there was such a thing as "Upstate New York" I still imagined the entire state as a busy concrete jungle.

The part of New York we entered was far from what I expected. Fields of corn grew between thick groves of trees, and not a single tall building was in sight. In fact, the only buildings I saw were modest farm homes and large adjoining barns. We were headed to our first course to film in Syracuse, but took a detour. Trevor really wanted a real shower after nearly a week without one, so we needed to stay in a campground, not a parking lot. We found one in Unadilla, which was about an hour off our planned route to Syracuse. We usually tried not to detour so far, especially with our poor gas mileage, but I wasn't complaining. The campground and its showers were well worth the extra gasoline we had to use to get there.

We hadn't thought to grab any food on our way to the campground in the middle of empty farmland, so we each had an apple for dinner and nothing else. If we had been desperately hungry, we could have cooked up some plain brown rice, but that just didn't sound very appetizing.

Without eating anything for breakfast the next morning, we continued on our way to Syracuse. When we approached the large town in Upstate New York, there were a lot of cars on the road. I started to become nervous about filming in all that traffic. But as we turned off on some smaller roads towards the lake where the course started, traffic seemed to disappear.

As we drove thirty miles per hour down the winding farm roads, where speed limits were only thirty-five or forty, no more than five cars passed us in total. It may have been the one filming day with the least amount of traffic out of them all. Still, in true New York fashion, it was also the only course where we got honked at as angry drivers passed us, barely going faster than we were.

On a tight schedule, we immediately left Syracuse and headed straight for our next filming destination: Lake Placid. There was something about the name of the city that struck me. I knew I had heard of Lake Placid before, but I couldn't remember where.

There was an importance surrounding the city name, and I became frustrated trying to remember why. I became even more frustrated when my iPhone's lack of signal refused to tell me why "Lake Placid" was famous.

After several hours of driving on two-lane county highways and winding mountain roads surrounded by tall trees and rivers, we arrived in the quaint mountain town. We slowly drove into the most adorable and picturesque downtown area. Despite the large lake that the city rested on, the town looked out of place in the summer. The architecture all around the town screamed "winter-time" and begged to be covered in blankets of fluffy, white snow.

As we reached the end of the main street, it struck me why the town sounded famous. We found a place to park so that we could explore a little, and the first building we passed was an Olympic stadium. Lake Placid was the home of the winter Olympics in 1932 and more recently in 1980, one of only four cities to hold the winter games twice. *That* was why it had sounded familiar.

After marveling at the building and the decades-old crumbling statues surrounding it, we headed to a Starbucks down the road. We had to charge all of the remotes and cameras yet again, plus export all of our Syracuse footage so we could film the course at Lake Placid in the morning.

Unable to find a Wal-Mart or a truck stop nearby, we were forced to sleep illegally in a local grocery store parking lot. After spending many nights in parking lots we weren't supposed to, I hardly felt like a vandal anymore. We were just doing what we needed to do. We would only be parked there for seven or eight hours; enough time to sleep and then we would be out before anyone was even awake and traveling to work.

The next morning we experienced some of the most beautiful country I had ever seen. During our filming in Lake Placid, I tried to keep my eyes on the blinking lights of the remotes to make sure our cameras stayed running, but it was difficult. I wanted to ogle the scenery going by and found myself gazing out the window for too many minutes at a time. Much of the course we were filming traversed alongside a crystal clear river, specked with round granite boulders. If there was any course I actually enjoyed filming, it was that one. Mostly because of the stunning location, but also because we were so good at filming by then that it wasn't as stressful as it used to be.

As always, we finished filming two hours later and were back where we had started. After we parked to take the cameras down, I expected us to get in the van to head towards Vermont, but Trevor had another plan. He was intrigued by the Olympic center and suggested we check it out.

We parked illegally (I know, and *still* no tickets) in the stadium's empty employee-only lot, then walked in a huge circle around the building, trying to find the entrance. There were about ten doors all around the front of the building that formed a half-circle, but all were locked. We almost gave up on trying the rest of the identical entrances, but then we saw a group of people come out of the farthest set of doors.

When we went through the unlocked doors, we were *not* greeted by a giant ice rink or hockey stadium, which is what I was expecting. Instead, we found ourselves in a small ten-foot by ten-foot foyer room. Three sides of the room each had one door; one we had just entered from, one was for tours, and one was unlabeled. The fourth side of the room without a door had a stairway instead.

Aside from that, there were no signs, arrows, maps or anything to suggest where to go. We picked the simplest option, and headed up the stairs.

Trevor and I tend to be very bad tourists because we are always in a hurry and never have enough time to really appreciate a place, whether it's a town, an event, or even something as simple as a monument. When we entered the Olympic stadium, it was by Trevor's request, and not mine. Usually, I'm the one dragging him hastily around all the places I want to see. This time, it was Trevor who seemed drawn in by the mystique of such an important, historic building.

When we got upstairs, we were completely enamored with the whole thing. Being a lover of architecture and physical places, I first studied the building and asked myself questions about it. How long had it taken to build and how many people could it hold? At the 1980 games, how many people walked through here? When we got to the end of that particular hall, we turned into another, which happened to be the Hall of Fame. That's when I stopped caring about the building and realized Trevor hadn't been interested in it at all. He was staring up at the black and white photos of skiers, skaters, and all-around amazing athletes. Some of the photos were from the 1932 games, while others were from the more recent ones. Still more photos were of local athletes that had competed all around the globe, adding medals to the legendary name of the small town that was Lake Placid.

Each photo was accompanied by a story. While each story was different, they all had two things in common. First, every story ended in a gold, silver, or bronze medal. Second, every story told a tale of adversity that the athlete had faced. Some grew up without families and sought refuge in the love of their sport. Some only had time to practice during certain months of the year when they weren't away for school. Others had contended at many Olympic games across the world and brought home a medal only when they got to compete in the comfort of their hometown.

No matter what the instance was, not one of these superior athletes had an easy path to the top of their sport. To me, that was even more inspiring than the amount of medals they had received. To be able to triumph so greatly in the face of any hardship is something that defines all of the greatest athletes in the world. I knew it was something that clicked with Trevor. We had faced our own fair share of difficulties already and it was important to remember we weren't alone in that. *It almost wouldn't be fair to make it to the top without having seemingly impossible challenges thrown in the way.*

Carefully Weigh All Options - Trevor

There was something special about our short stay in Upstate New York. Perhaps it was the unexpected peacefulness of the endless green mountains. Or, perhaps it was simply the historical significance of this part of the country.

As we got closer to the New England area, you could almost feel the famous and daring past all around. This land belonged to the dreamers. First claimed by people who risked it all in hopes of a better life. Then, people whose bravery far exceeded their fear of failure transformed it into the United States of America. Our Founding Fathers fought, against all odds, to create not only the freest country in the world with quite literally endless opportunities, but they also provided an eternal message to the world. *No challenge is insurmountable when you have a purpose, dream, and are ready for a relentless pursuit.*

Still, I often hear people claim that the American Dream is dead. There's a lot of pessimism in the world and to be quite honest, it's understandable. Our society puts so much pressure on young people to immediately jump into whichever line of work has open positions or pays the best. Filling up a bank account becomes first priority. We are convinced that we need lavish commodities like cars, boats, and jewelry in order to achieve "success."

With this in mind, young graduates are forced down this inevitably unfulfilling path of working towards money, rather than working towards a purpose. A kid who spent his entire childhood wanting to make a difference will one day give up in exchange for a much simpler and unfulfilling path to money. Still, there is no amount of zeros in a bank account that could make up for a life lived without purpose and passion.

To me, the American Dream is more alive than ever. Technology advances have shrunk the world and created more opportunities right now domestically and internationally than ever before. They might seem a little different than they once did but they require the same creativity, courage and hard work.

The truth is, the world is in need of dreamers and entrepreneurs more than ever before. The biggest problems on the planet today need people brave enough to stray from the beaten path and dedicate their entire lives to finding a solution and bettering the world. The people who will become successful are those who are passionate about chasing something bigger than themselves.

As we crossed a massive bridge over the skinny southern tip of Lake Champlain, Vermont awaited on the other side. While the mood remained tense and focused from Nationals, the flowing farm roads of this new and magnificent land seemed to bring both of us back down to earth. The many complexities of the week prior had managed to cover up the sheer beauty of the East Coast and of the entire adventure. Fortunately, Vermont was quick to remind us.

The first stop was Burlington, Vermont, which was about fifteen minutes away from the race venue. As usual, we were planning to stay in the Wal-Mart parking lot for the several days leading up to the race. Burlington is the largest city in Vermont, but the population of 42,000 isn't even a fifth of that of Reno. Still, there were ten times as many healthy food options and fitness centers than we had back home. On top of this, the people are fantastic. In classic "happy mountain person" fashion, just about everyone was kind, fit, and incredibly enthusiastic about the outdoors. I was in paradise.

The first night at the Burlington Wal-Mart, I decided to do a quick TrainerRoad ride to spin out my restless legs from the drive that day. I set up my riding station outside the open doors of the van like I had been doing all trip, and got to work. As the sun began to set, the temperature dropped to a slightly chilly level. As I went through my workout intervals, the lower temperature felt refreshing. Unfortunately, I wasn't the only one who thought so.

With the sun almost completely submerged behind the green mountains, I started noticing several small bugs attempting to land on my sweaty arms. My workout was starting to heat up so I just brushed them off and didn't think too much of it.

Then, all of a sudden, Sierra jumped out of the van, where she had been bundled up and peacefully working. Once out, she began slapping herself uncontrollably as she danced around in the parking lot in frustration. Confused, I pulled my headphones out, stopped pedaling and asked what was wrong, urging her to calm down. Without saying a word, she managed to briefly stop beating herself and pointed to the inside of the van as she continued to dance around.

Now worried, I hopped off my bike and asked her again what was the matter. This time, she replied, in between labored breathing from dancing around so rigorously, "So. Many. Mosquitoes!"

By now, it was completely dark. The only light was coming from my laptop screen. Assuming Sierra was being a little dramatic, I opened the second side door, triggering the dome light inside of the van to illuminate. The sight I saw was something straight out of a horror movie.

Glowing in the light just below the ceiling in the van was a massive swarm of mosquitoes. There were hundreds. No, there were thousands. The cloud of small bugs was so thick it morphed the view to the dome light. I jumped back at first, shocked at what I was looking at. *We had to sleep in there.*

Sweaty and dumbfounded, all I could do was stare into the van in amazement. In the forty-five minutes I had had the door open while I did my workout, the van had completely filled with mosquitoes to almost an imaginary level. Sierra had been so deeply focused on her work while the sound of my bike drowned out the disgustingly loud and high pitched buzz, she hadn't realized the extent of the invasion.

I quickly opened the back of the van, ripped off my riding clothes and loaded my bike and trainer up. Next, Sierra and I covered ourselves in bug spray and as many clothes as we could. The mosquitoes were not going to willingly leave our van and we knew it. We only had one option and that was to *make* them leave.

With several layers of clothes on to hopefully protect us from bites, we reluctantly entered the van, shut all of the windows so no more could enter, and got to work. Swatting and bashing all about for well over an hour, we tried to exterminate the bloodsucking cloud before it feasted on us once we went to bed. Knowing full well it would be impossible to get rid of all of them, it was all about damage control at this point.

When we finally couldn't hear the awful buzz of flying mosquitoes any longer, we began setting up our bedroom, still on high alert for flying enemies. I was a little warm and sweaty from my ride and the stressful mosquito war, but I knew that shedding a single layer before going to sleep was not an option. There were plenty more mosquitoes hiding out in the van and it would only be a matter of time before they got hungry and came out of hiding. So, Sierra and I scrunched ourselves down into our small sleeping hole that held the air mattress and forced our eyes closed, hoping the warm and uncomfortable night would be over shortly.

We were both relieved when morning arrived. We had survived the night behind enemy lines. I felt dehydrated from the constant sweat I had going on since the night before, but being uncomfortable was something we were both pretty used to at this point.

After a quick trip to the grocery store, we headed out to the race venue to check out the course. In classic VanLife style, we were planning on just living in the parking area at the race for the next two days, so we needed to stock up on meals.

The race venue was incredible. It was an unbelievably fun network of trails through a giant, grass field and up into some of the thickly wooded hills that surrounded the open space. There were plenty of manmade features including berms, rock gardens, jumps, and big drops. Still, none of the technical sections in Vermont came close to the massive drop that I had tackled in Montana.

I was able to get all of the technical lines figured out on the first lap and then I spent the rest of the day enjoying the remarkably fun Vermont riding. While focus and determination still remained from the hardship in Pennsylvania, I was having a blast just riding my bike.

When Friday rolled around I started the day off with another couple of laps around the four-mile course. As I went out on my third time around, I was really starting to feel the flow. The course just meshed so well with me, which was a great sign for the race the next day. I hit all of the A-lines flawlessly time and time again.

Then, on my final lap for the day, something happened. As I touched down after the final big drop, I heard and felt something on my bike crunch. I slammed on the brakes and jumped off to assess the damage. Strangely, I didn't see anything. I didn't even see any rocks or logs nearby that could have flung up to hit the bike. This would have been the only logical explanation to the noise since it had been a smooth landing.

Confused, I hopped back on my bike, hoping I had just been wrong about the sound, but as soon as I pushed down on a pedal, I knew that I hadn't been wrong. The large bearing inside the bottom of the frame where the arms that hold the pedals go into the bike was annihilated. It had completely exploded, and the bike needed to be repaired in order to be rideable.

Further, the bearings in this level of bike are not only extremely expensive, but also nearly impossible to find. These bearings are supposed to be bulletproof, so stocking such an expensive, rarely used part doesn't make sense for bike shops.

After making a few phone calls, I found out that it would be at least ten days before I would be able to get a replacement.

The damage had taken place on my full suspension bike, which was by far my weapon of choice for the rocky and root-y racecourse in Vermont. However, given the circumstances, my other bike with only front suspension would have to suffice. I had no time to be bummed out about the situation, nor would it do me any good. My hardtail race bike was an incredible machine, and I refused to let the sudden change of plans take away from my focus going into the weekend.

When Saturday arrived, I got up a little earlier than planned to take my hardtail bike out for a quick ride and get used to it again. I had been riding my full suspension bike all week, so I wanted to adjust to the more rigid hardtail before the race got started.

With the North American World Cup just a week away in Quebec (about three hours from Burlington), there was an incredible international showing at the final Pro XCT that day. This race was a perfect way for international pros to get acquainted with the North American lifestyle and terrain before the enormously competitive World Cup events. As the best from around the world mingled around the start/finish area and talked with their mechanics about the course, I headed out for an easy lap.

Though I still would have preferred my full suspension bike, the course turned out to be great for a hardtail. The extra stiffness the bike provided seemed to work perfectly around the course and in some of the huge berms and jumps.

Then, as I exited one of the rock gardens, I heard a familiar crunching sound. My heart sunk. "Maybe it was just a rock flying up and lightly hitting the bike," I tried to convince myself as I skidded to a halt.

As I looked the bike over, there was no visible damage….again. Knowing exactly what had happened but in complete denial, I gritted my teeth and hopped back on the bike. As I pushed down to make the first pedal stroke back down the course, *the whole world might as well have come crashing down around me.*

The bearings in this bike had gone out, too. This time, in an even more incredible fashion, damaging other parts of the bike along with it. The odds of such a catastrophic mechanical problem occurring on both bikes in the same weekend was next to none. Having just gone through the same situation the day before, I knew there was no easy solution to this now devastating predicament.

Shaking with anger, disappointment, and confusion, I rolled my bike back to the van. Sierra had been out on the course taking photos, but she quickly met me and my broken bikes back at our little camp in the parking lot, wondering why I had never made it to her position on the course.

It was over. That was all I could think. We had come this far, and now I had finally gotten myself into a situation I couldn't get out of. The only option was to give up.

As the racing got underway, I wallowed in disbelief and disappointment back at the van. I hadn't even taken my helmet off as I sat, staring at my disabled bikes.

Without saying a word, Sierra brought over the solar shower filled with freezing cold water from the bike wash at the end of the parking lot. I grabbed the tarp from the storage container on top of the van, built a small shelter for privacy, and took a frigid shower. The numbing cold seemed to clear my mind just slightly. Sierra noticed the opportunity and began talking with me about the terrible situation.

Three thousand miles away from home on a mountain bike race tour, with no bikes to ride. Pretty awful, right? I made a few more phone calls to see if there was any chance we could salvage anything, but the best anyone could do was have parts sent out to me in about ten days, if I was lucky. Then, I would have to find a shop somewhere that was able to press the new bearings into the bike and fix the damage the exploded ones had made. All the while, I would be missing the first North American World Cup in Quebec, which was just five days away. Also, I would be extremely close to missing the final World Cup in New York that we had on the schedule, which was just eleven days away.

The thought of waiting around, sleeping in parking lots for almost two more weeks just to have my parts arrive a day late, forcing me to miss the last race made me sick. Even worse would be to receive the parts on time the day before the race, but not be able to find someone to properly install them before the event. This option just didn't seem smart.

I made a few more phone calls, describing the situation to some more of my sponsors and supporters back home. While racing the World Cups had always been more of an experience-building bonus to this entire tour, the final Pro XCT had been so much more. I had been fighting my way through the ranks all summer and was so close to putting in the results I knew I was capable of. Further, I was so close to putting in the results I knew I *needed* in order to secure the best sponsorships and funding going into the next year. All of that seemed to be gone now.

Then, almost jokingly, a friend from Specialized reminded me that the All-Mountain World Championships just so happened to be going on the weekend after the Vermont race in Downieville, California. California also just so happened to be where my parts were, sitting safely inside the Specialized warehouse. Unknowingly, he had just sparked a fire of inspiration inside of me.

With the World Cup events that I was planning to race being entirely cross-country focused, the race in Downieville was more catered to the mountain bike racer who loved speed. Yes, the event did contain a massive climb, but it also had a twenty-mile, world-famous descent. The idea behind the All-Mountain World Championships was to test every aspect of a mountain bike racer's skills. From climbing to descending, to become an All-Mountain World Champ, you had to be able to do a lot more than just pedal a bike.

Rather than waiting and hoping for a miracle to race one final race in New York, I was contemplating taking destiny into my own hands, loading up the van, and driving to Downieville. It would require over fifty hours of driving in less than seven days, but I could pick up parts and get my bike fixed by Specialized along the way. Then, I could race a true West Coast event, which I was so accustomed to, and still keep my hopes alive of putting in some jaw-dropping results and landing myself the best possible support for the next season.

The idea was nearly impossible, just by the logistics. Driving that much in that short of time was nuts. On top of that, I would still have to remain fit and competitive in order to race well in Downieville and that would only matter if my bike repairs went smoothly and without issue. Oh, and remember that time the van almost caught on fire in Montana? The thought of a three thousand-mile straight shot across the continent and what it might do to our silver stallion made my stomach turn. Still, this was my best shot at getting one more opportunity to compete against the top mountain bikers in the world. Plus, I knew the race at Downieville suited my skills very well.

Sierra and I extensively discussed the pros and cons of both options. With the final Pro XCT in Vermont now out of the question as well as the first of the two North American World Cups gone due to the time frame of my parts arriving, the decision came down to two options: We could wait in New York for the final World Cup and hope my parts arrived the day before the event like they were tentatively scheduled to. Then, we would have to hope we could find a suitable bike shop in time to get them installed correctly.

The other option was to head to the All-Mountain World Championships on the other side of the country. I could pick up parts from Specialized on the way, as long as we made it to California in time, and be able to race the infamous Downieville event. While neither option guaranteed success, at least the latter of the two was more in my control. The thought of waiting hopelessly in New York for parts that may or may not arrive in time made me sick. So, we made the decision to load up the van and head to Cali. It was a long shot, but it was still a shot. *There was no time to waste.*

Part 6 – Going for Broke

Make Your Own Luck - Sierra

Nothing ever stays the same. In every aspect of life, things are always changing. People change, places change, and plans change. It is completely inevitable and unavoidable. Sometimes we are ready for it; we plan for it and embrace it. Other times change comes unannounced, rearranging your expectations. When it does that, there's nothing you can do but make the most of the necessary adjustments. In the end, it might even turn out for the better.

We sat in silence as we drove into the afternoon sun, leaving Vermont with a sudden change of plans. Aside from the small jaunt on I-80 in Pennsylvania a few days prior, we hadn't traveled westward in a very long time. We were used to traveling with the sun behind us, and now it was blinding us with a burst of yellow-orange rays. The silence in the van wasn't uncomfortable. Instead, it felt like the kind of necessary silence you pay when someone is singing the national anthem. As if we were driving in silence as a sign of respect for our colossal undertaking.

I wasn't sure what was going through Trevor's mind at this point. He had a mix of sternness, thoughtfulness, and wonder all blending together across his face like a watercolor painting. I wanted to ask him what he was thinking, but at the same time I wasn't sure if he would even hear me. He was so deep in thought where I couldn't reach him.

Trying to keep the mood as positive as it could be despite the surprise decision to head west, I pointed at herds of cows and sheep roaming the rural New York landscape we were now in. Sometimes Trevor smiled meekly at my efforts, while other times he just shot a glance out the window before resuming his intense state of concentration.

233

We were somewhere in the middle of New York when the sun began setting in front of us. A large, crisp cloud broke the light and sent sun rays shooting upwards and outwards, so that they made a windmill in the sky. The colors were just as unreal.

We put another audiobook on, this time trying a little harder to follow the plot line and stay interested. I wasn't sure how far we would make it that night, but I knew I needed to stay awake to help keep Trevor alert and awake, or at least I wanted to. He was great at driving long hours, never becoming too sleepy to be dangerous. Me, on the other hand, I had begun to doze off at the drop of a hat, as the weight of this trip pushed down on me the more we traveled. It was a good thing I didn't have to drive.

We spent the night at a truck stop just inside the eastern Ohio border. I was so tired by the time we stopped sometime after midnight, I don't even remember blowing up the air mattress. We set our alarms but when 6 a.m. rolled around and they started beeping, we both turned them off without giving it another thought.

Finally, I woke up three hours later, in a slight panic because I knew we had slept much longer than planned. Every extra hour we spent sleeping was another hour we could be driving towards California. An hour could mean the difference between making it to the bike shop before it closed or not. An hour could mean the difference between having a fixed bike to race and having no bike at all.

I wasn't even sure where we were in Ohio. I had stopped paying attention to the highway signs once it had gotten dark. All I knew was there was a gas station and Denny's outside in the center of the parking lot. We were surrounded by several motorhomes on the edges of the lot. Aside from the freeway, there was nothing else in sight.

I shook Trevor awake, and his eyes opened with a strained look, like he hadn't gotten much sleep at all. The previous day had taken a lot out of him, I was sure, so I couldn't blame him for the distressed look. We had driven twelve hours the previous night and we needed to drive at least eighteen that day.

When we remembered that we needed to feed ourselves, we sighed at our options. We could try to find something worthwhile at the gas station store; probably some string cheese and an overly ripe banana, or we could have Denny's. I hadn't been to Denny's in a long time because I really wasn't a fan. Had we had any other options, I would have chosen them without a second thought. Unfortunately, we just didn't have any alternatives.

We were seated in a booth with ripped plastic seats, furthering my disapproval of the establishment. I sat across from Trevor and inspected just how filthy he looked. He had dirt rubbed across his forehead and cheeks, and he still had lines on his face from sleeping on his pillowcase, apparently without moving. His eyes were red from stress and traveling, and were pointed aimlessly at the table. I giggled when he absentmindedly tried to reach for the straw in his water cup without looking at it. He missed several times before snapping back to life and pulling the straw to his mouth.

After picking through a predictably unappetizing breakfast of burnt bacon, greasy eggs, and even greasier hash browns, we got back on the road, heading west. That second day of driving was a complete blur. We had our new audiobook on; one that I was actually excited to listen to. As the book played over the speakers, I visualized the scenes in my head so vividly that I no longer saw through the windshield. The land outside was flat and monotonous, anyway.

We gave up on avoiding toll roads and just tried to get to Downieville as soon as possible to ensure the bikes were fixed in time. We went through state after state, unceremoniously passing colorful welcome signs and paying their tolls.

"Welcome to Indiana! Crossroads of America."

"Welcome to Illinois! The Land of Lincoln."

"The People of Iowa Welcome You. Iowa, Fields of Opportunities."

Chapters of the audiobook went by. Endless fields of corn went by. The sun went up and over us and eventually it went by, too. We reached Nebraska in the dark and then drove as long as Trevor could stand to before pulling into a truck stop in the middle of nowhere. After sleeping for about six hours, we groggily crawled into the gas station store to find something that might pass for breakfast. We grabbed some cups of coffee that tasted more like stale water and dirt than the delicious coffee we were used to drinking from the Hub Coffee Roasters back in Reno.

Actually, pretty much all of the coffee we had drank on the trip tasted bland and wrong in comparison to Hub coffee. Trevor had been good friends with the owner of the Hub, Mark, for quite some time. Mark even donated his top-of-the-line coffee to Trevor's junior team to sell as a fundraiser. He was exactly the kind of entrepreneur we admired and sought inspiration from.

You see, Mark doesn't just own a coffee shop. It goes much deeper than that. Without knowing much about Mark's background, I do know that if you catch him during a moment that he's able to sit down and chat, his absolute favorite thing to talk about is coffee. From the different regions it is grown to the science behind the variety of flavors the roasting process can bring out in a blend, coffee is an art form to Mark. *It is an art that his entire life revolves around.*

Mark is so dedicated to his passion for coffee that he travels the world in search of only the best coffee growers, makes deals with them, and has their coffee shipped straight to him to roast to perfection in Reno. It's an absolutely amazing feat. And to think, he built his roastery in the height of the recession, not the best of moves financially. But Mark's desire to provide the best coffee to the Reno area and beyond trumped everyone's disbelief. Now? Now, Mark has two thriving coffee shops in town along with the roastery and is in the process of opening up several other shops in Nevada and beyond. *His work ethic, combined with his passion for and dedication to coffee is what has made him so successful.* He is the epitome of the entrepreneurs that Trevor and I strive to be and to top it off, we thoroughly love his coffee.

Despite the state being so large, Nebraska also flew passed our windows without much notice on the third day of driving. It was more of the same landscape we had witnessed for the entire day before. I continued to stare out into the plains and get lost in our increasingly odd and interesting audiobook.

It was a cheesy sci-fi and not my first choice in reading material, but the spider-aliens in the book intrigued me. They were more interesting than watching corn go by, at least. They were also less stressful than worrying whether we would even make it to Downieville or not.

We still had a few days, but we had to figure out if Trevor's bikes would be fixed before we got to the race. On top of that, Trevor had acquired a small cold, and we weren't sure if he would be well enough to race by the weekend. A lot had to go right for this to work. No one could guarantee we would make it.

Still, Trevor was holding it together well. I always admired his ability to see things for what they were. Sometimes, it's hard to see the positive side in a negative situation, but together we always manage to find it. That's what this trip to California now was. It was the one positive in the list of negatives we had recently encountered, and we had to see it through. Without a positive mindset, our adventure would have stopped being "adventurous" long ago. Instead, it would have been a chore. *Not everything goes the way you plan and we had definitely learned and accepted that. We knew that there was no point in wallowing over unfortunate circumstances.*

As we reached Wyoming, now for the third time that summer, our book stopped playing. There was probably only one chapter left, but our phones couldn't find enough service to download it. We were left wondering where the aliens came from and whether or not our main character was going to live. At least Wyoming is pretty enough that I could keep entertained just by watching the mountains go by. Being back in the West filled me with all new excitement for adventures yet to come.

I was returning a different person than when I had left and that was one thing to be happy about. I had already learned so much from our experiences living on the road. Just as I had wanted from the beginning, I was being tested in more ways than I could imagine. Our journey so far had been thrilling, but it had also been full of challenges. A lot of these challenges would have sent me running, years ago. Now, I was learning to embrace them and allow them to build and shape me into a better person.

Through all of the difficulties Trevor and I had faced so far, I was becoming stronger in facing them. I think Trevor was, too. There is no avoiding adversity, but you can make it work in your favor. You can let it mold and sharpen you. You can accept that it happens and laugh in the face of it, rather than cower. These are the things I was learning and looking at my life, it was only just the beginning of an extraordinary journey.

Have Faith - Trevor

I can't explain the feeling I got when we crossed over the Nevada border and back into our home state. Physically, I was numb. My body was on cruise control as I sat in the driver's seat of the van for literally days on end. Emotionally, I tried my best to also be numb. The fact of the matter was, I didn't want to be back in Nevada. Our early arrival to the barren, wide-open desert was not in the plans. While normally I can find comfort and beauty in the dry Nevada landscape, this time I was fighting off feelings of anger and despair.

It was still another five hours before we would see the bright lights of Reno, but I just wanted to hurry up and get the experience of prematurely being home over with. I wanted to blaze straight through as if I hadn't been there at all. Had we not been so short on time, I would have taken a detour up into Idaho, over to Oregon, and then down into California. All of that, just to avoid returning to Nevada two weeks earlier than we had planned.

I knew the circumstances for our premature departure for the West Coast were completely out of my hands. I also knew that the reason I was back was because I wanted to actively maintain control over my destiny, rather than hope for a miracle while waiting around aimlessly on the East Coast. Still, my mind had a very difficult time differentiating between failure and change.

I've spent countless nights, tossing and turning, debating this very topic in my mind since our great journey. If this was just change, what would constitute failure? My endless nights of reflection have led me to this conclusion – *the difference between failure and change is in the intentions behind them.* I didn't set out to win a World Cup.

I didn't set out to win a Pro XCT. In fact, I didn't set out for any specific race results. I started this entire journey in order to take the first steps in becoming one of the best North American mountain bike racers. Pro XCT races and World Cups are certainly great events to pursue a goal like this. However, they definitely aren't the only way to the top. Many legends of the sport have proven this.

When I was faced with an insurmountable obstacle in Vermont, I didn't give up on reaching the top of my sport. Giving up on this would have been failure. Instead, I looked for the next best route to my ultimate destination. *I changed the plan, not the goal.*

When we finally made it to Reno, the sun had long set. As if we were strangers to the little mountain town nestled in the foothills of the Sierra Nevada Mountains, we drove straight through, giving it no more than a passing glance. It was several more hours until we would be at the Specialized shop in California. On top of this, it was guaranteed that the shop would be closed at such a ridiculous hour of the night. Still, I refused to leave anything to chance. We had come way too far to let anything get in the way.

Aside from one last fuel stop, the van would not be shifted into "park" until we were safe and sound in the parking lot outside of the shop. We had quite literally traveled from coast to coast in three days. Against all odds, we had made it to exactly where we needed to be and right on time. As I turned the ignition off and pulled the key out, I sat for just a second staring in awe up at the red Specialized sign on top of the building. My bloodshot eyes burned with exhaustion and spine ached from the lack of mobility for three days. Before sliding to the back of the van to begin setting up the air mattress, I rubbed the dash and quietly said "thank you" to our van. *We made it.*

With only a handful of hours of sleep, the moment the sun hit the side of the van, I immediately woke up. Our poor curtains had become so haggard that they barely provided any shielding of the windows anymore. Any ray of light from the outside world and the inside of our metal home was immediately illuminated. While this was quite irritating on most days when I was uninterested at getting up at the crack of dawn, I was thankful for it on this day.

The last thing standing between myself and racing the All-Mountain World Championships in Downieville in just a few more days was my equipment. I only needed one bike to be in working condition so that I could race, but there was no guarantee that would be possible. The extent of the damage was unknown before we had arrived at the shop. If it was just the bearings, I would be fine. However, if there was something else, the three-day, brutal sprint across North America would have been all for nothing.

Sitting with my bikes in front of the shop, I waited for somebody to come and open the doors. Fortunately, it wasn't a long wait as the mechanic had been expecting me and came in early. There was no messing around as he opened the doors, threw my bike on a stand, and got to work.

The job took all of an hour to complete. Once the bike was back together, he handed it to me for a quick test ride. As I hopped on, he explained that it didn't look like there was any other damage, and it came together very smoothly. *Finally, some good news.* My bike was good. I cruised around the parking lot a few times, but I could immediately tell. While my hardtail would have to remain broken in the van for another week, my full suspension bike was now ready to race and that was all that mattered. I would get the other bike fixed when we got home.

Leaving the shop, we went deeper into the California mountains to the small town of Sierra City, which is just twelve miles away from Downieville. The legendary, point-to-point race that makes up the All-Mountain World Championships starts here, climbs a giant mountain, and then descends into Downieville.

Now that the unknown of whether or not I was even going to have the opportunity to race had passed, my mind began to hone in on a whole new set of issues. The majority of these issues centered on just how gnarly this race is. Downieville is a race that professional mountain bike racers will prepare for all year long. Some of the best all-mountain riders in the world will spend weeks in the small mining town in the hills of California, studying every inch of the course. They do this partly to find faster routes down the trails, but also to find safer ones. Even the amateur racers will come up a few times before the event in order to scout out the best lines over the rocky, unforgiving trails. While my home in Reno was only a state away, I had never ridden in Downieville, nor did I know exactly what to expect.

Once I knew for sure that I was racing, the unknown and treacherous terrain worried me a little. Even more, the thin mountain air really worried me. Having spent the last month and a half at sea level, the 7,500-foot mountain the course climbs over was going to be brutal. Still, I was relieved to even be able to race. I finally felt like I had made the right decision back in Vermont and regardless of my challenging circumstances, at least I had another shot.

I cruised around through the mountains a little bit on Thursday and Friday before the race to try and loosen up my body. The massive amounts of driving had really left my muscles and joints tight and sore. While the twenty-eight-mile, point-to-point racecourse was way too long to pre-ride without fatiguing myself, the mountainous dirt roads were plenty to get my heart rate up.

I wasn't feeling great going into the race. The cold I had began to come down with while driving during the week had worsened slightly. The thin, dry mountain air seemed to be unable to fill my lungs like the thick, dense air in Vermont had. I also had been living off of a steady diet of gas station coffee and trail mix since we left the East Coast with no training at all. *This was going to be tough.*

The course in Downieville consists of a massive 4,000-foot, eight-mile climb. Next is a 5,500-foot, twenty-mile descent. Having never even ridden in the area before, I knew it would be difficult for me to make up a lot of time on the descent, where the speeds and stakes are high. Instead, my plan was to get all of my work done on the climb. While the top cross-country riders were at the World Cup on the East Coast that weekend, I was confident I would be one of, if not *the* strongest rider on the climb. I knew I wouldn't be the fastest on the long and brutal descent, but I wouldn't have to be if I had a big enough lead going over the top of the mountain. I would simply have to hold it together and ride smoothly until the finish.

Race day rolled around, and Sierra and I were now pros when it came to the VanLife morning race ritual. The Sierra Nevada air was chilly as we cooked breakfast and transformed our bedroom back into a living room by folding up our blanket and air mattress. As I rolled through town for my warm up, I continued to see familiar faces light up with shock and excitement to see me back in California. Sierra and I had been so focused on the situation at hand, we hadn't told a single person of the sudden change of plans and coasts. So many of my friends and fans were on the West Coast and had made the trip to Downieville for the legendary event. Being able to race in front of them again was fantastic and served as a great motivator.

As staging began, I noticed the majority of my competitors had massive tires on their bikes. The thick, burly tread reminded me of a dirt bike tire. While I had put some thicker, tougher tires on my bike as well the day before, they were nothing like the ones my competitors had on. It was as if they were ready to go race through a minefield. Obviously they knew something I didn't.

They began calling the top ranked riders to the line. I was confident I would be starting from the back since I had never done this event before and Pro XCT points were useless there. Then I heard my name being yelled from the front line of racers. It was a friend of mine who rides for the bike manufacturer Santa Cruz, and had landed himself on the podium at this very event the year before. He was yelling to me, telling me to come to the front. He had convinced the official in charge of staging that I deserved to be up there, and I was able to sneak my way up to the second row. Things were already off to a good start.

As I waited for the start gun to go off, I spent just a second taking it all in. Somehow, we successfully traveled over 3,000 miles in a matter of days. We had gambled and won. Yes, I still had to race and finish well for it to really be a success, but just having the opportunity to go to battle with the top riders in the world once more that summer was a win in and of itself.

Pop! Smoke shot out of the gun, and we were off. Being used to the cross-country sprint races that were the Pro XCT's, the initial pace of the race seemed strangely easy. It was as if everyone was just pacing themselves for the day ahead.

The first half-mile of the climb to the top of the mountain was on pavement. I took advantage of the easy pace to move up right behind the lead rider. I settled in behind him, comfortably waiting for somebody to make a move to get away from the pack. Not knowing the climb or the race in general, I decided to wait patiently, rather than making a run for it alone.

As the climb turned to a rough and rocky dirt road, we popped out of the tree coverage. Now fully exposed to the blazing morning sun, I knew heat and dehydration were possible if I exerted myself too hard. Though the pace of the rider I was following didn't increase, I felt my body start to heat up as sweat began to flow freely from my face and into my eyes. It burned, but I couldn't afford to let my focus waiver, as I was now struggling to stay with the lead rider.

Half way into the climb, I looked back to assess what damage awaited if I were to fall off the pace a bit. To my surprise, there wasn't another rider in sight. The leader and myself had dropped everyone. Knowing this, I eased up on the pedals just enough to feel comfortable.

The leader began to inch away, but I was confident I would be seeing him again shortly on the descent. In a controversial appearance, the rider who was now pulling away from me was a very famous, former road cyclist whose career had ended when he was busted for taking performance-enhancing drugs. I was very aware of who he was and of his history the second I saw him on the starting line. I think just about every rider there knew, and it was just added motivation.

Like myself, so many young professional mountain bike racers are working every single day for a spot at the top of the sport. This road rider had been at the top of the sport. In fact, he is extremely wealthy and now spends his days doing whatever he pleases (like mountain biking) due to the fortune he made from cheating. While others, including myself, fight tooth and nail just to get enough cash to make it to the races, he lives a life of luxury. Calling him a "cheat" or a "doper" was one way many chose to deal with it. But those of us on the line with him just wanted to beat him.

As I crested the top of the mountain, the leader was now out of sight. With his background being in road cycling and mine in moto, I was confident I could catch him, even without knowing the trails very well.

A few miles into the descent, a group of three riders caught me. In the group was legendary mountain bike racer and personal hero of mine, Carl Decker. Carl was the reigning champ of Downieville and had been crushing famous races like this since before I even knew what mountain biking was. With that kind of talent now in front of me, I did my best just to hold onto the pack and mimic the way they glided down the rocky trails at blistering speeds.

The descent was rough. It was steep and covered with huge, loose rocks. I was able to find a good rhythm and pace behind the incredible riders that were now just in front of me. While I knew it was still far from over, I began thinking about what an incredible story a fourth place finish at Downieville would make. Being kicked to the dirt and then making a cross-country journey on a thread of hope back to California to earn the best finish of my career. It would make for the perfect ending to the summer. *Unfortunately, life doesn't always follow the storyline you have in mind.*

As I ripped down one of the most high-speed sections of the course, I thought I felt my tire sealant spraying on the back of my legs. This was a sure sign that the tread had been ripped and that a flat was imminent. Flats were easy to fix, so I didn't panic. Instead, I looked down to confirm that it was in fact tire sealant hitting my legs and not just my imagination.

As soon as my eyes came off the rocky trail in front of me, my front wheel hit a massive hole and tucked. The world seemed to get stuck in slow motion as I ejected over my handlebars and down the mountain at about thirty-five miles per hour. The moment my body made contact with the small-boulders that covered the trail, a violent sequence of rolls and tumbles followed. The vicious impacts from cartwheeling down the mountain ripped off my right glove and my left shoe. When I finally came to a stop, I could barely make out my bike through the giant dust cloud, still tumbling end-over-end down the mountain. It finally came to a stop about fifty yards below me.

Laying in the rocks and dust, I took a quick second to take a mental inventory of my body. My knee and my gloveless hand were shrieking with pain, but I still had mobility in both. Knowing that the real pain was on its way once the adrenaline subsided, I picked myself up without hesitation. The index finger on my exposed hand was bent to the left and my knee was dripping blood down my leg. *"Just get back on the bike,"* I urged myself.

I began walking down the mountain to my bike, stumbling as my barefoot stepped on sharp rocks. My shoe had made it an additional fifteen feet down from where I had landed. I put it back on, but my glove was nowhere to be found.

When I arrived at my bike, the rear tire that I had thought was going flat, was in fact punctured and droopy. To my surprise, though, the rest of my bike seemed fine and completely rideable. While I knew my current physical state was going to make it extremely hard to maintain my podium position down the rest of the mountain, I had come way too far not to try. I had the supplies to fix one flat, which I did quickly beside the trail. Throughout the entire process, I had only lost a single position and was now pedaling back down the mountain.

My left hand was completely useless from the fall. Holding on was difficult and shifting and braking were out of the question. Each technical rocky section sent sharp jolts of pain into my knee and up through my body. With about six miles to go, I used every ounce of my will to just hold on.

The group I was initially descending with was now long gone. I found it extremely difficult to hold the pace they were going while riding alone. On top of that, I was simply struggling to hold onto my bike. As the miles went by, riders slipped around me one by one. I did my best to ignore my sudden change of fortune and just kept charging toward the finish.

Then, with about three miles left, my rear tire began to hiss, signaling another puncture. Still in a descent position and so close to the finish, I made one final push in an effort to cover the three miles before my tire lost all of its air. Like the thread of hope I was grasping so tightly to, the last bit of air slipped away and my rim hit the unforgiving, rocky dirt. *My race was done.*

I walked down the rest of the course, carrying my bicycle to save the now exposed carbon wheel from the rocky trail. The twenty-minute walk allowed for time to reflect on the almost ridiculous change in fortune that had occurred since the Pro XCT in Wisconsin. Sure, the silver medal in Super-D at Nationals was a small success, but the ocean of defeat surrounding it made it seem worthless.

I had gone to lengths that no other rider in the world had gone to in order to chase my dream. I hadn't slept in a real bed in months. I had spent thousands of dollars on fuel alone. I had given up a normal "college kid" summer, and for what? The culmination of all of the sacrifice and hardship was this agonizingly painful and tragic walk to the finish line for a close-to-last-place finish.

The days following Downieville were difficult. Very few words were spoken between Sierra and me. Very few words were spoken between myself and anyone for that matter. Finally being home and having simple luxuries like running water, a refrigerator, and a bed were nice but insignificant. While Sierra hadn't physically been on the bike with me, she felt the same pain I did. Emotionally, she had been on the exact same rollercoaster I was on. She had sacrificed just as much as I had and wanted some kind of reward for our efforts. Instead, the only benefit we received was the empty satisfaction of being back home.

Sure, the experience and personal growth from the incredible struggle was valuable. But it was almost impossible to validate the entire summer over something as abstract and intangible as "experience." I needed something more. I needed to know that everything we had gone through actually meant something. I needed some kind of reassurance that I was now closer to my goal of becoming a top professional mountain bike racer. Yet, the only thing I had at that moment was a sore and battered body and two mangled bicycles.

As I've stated before, I'm not the type of person who advocates idealistic, cliché lifestyles built upon the fallacy of my least favorite grade school quote –"If you can dream it, you can do it!" The fact is, dreaming it is only the start and most *can't* do it. Not because they are physically incapable or because their dream is just impossible. Rather, most people will never live their dreams because of the sickening amount of work required to blaze your own path in this world. Anything really worth achieving is going to be found on the other side of an obstacle that most would deem insurmountable.

Since the summer had ended in rather disastrous fashion, I certainly didn't have any big-name sponsors knocking down my door to sign me for the next season. While I knew my potential and I had shown a few small flashes of brilliance, my poor conclusion to the season seemed to completely eliminate me from anyone's radar.

I was willing to exhaust myself physically, emotionally, and financially for one summer in order to make it, but I didn't know if I was willing to do it again. Without any hope for increased support for the following season, it was a struggle to wrap my mind around the thought of starting over.

As our first week back home reached the end, I did my best to entirely avoid the topic of next season. It was something I was far from ready to discuss and I felt almost scared about what my decision towards it would be.

Sierra understood and spent the entire week seeking refuge from the depths of her laptop. While I sulked and reflected on the summer, she had been finishing up some of the biggest projects she had ever taken on for Blü World. What's even more impressive is that she had attained and managed the majority of the work while completely engulfed in our VanLife endeavors and I was not even aware of it.

Back in January of that year, I remember sitting down with her to set some different goals for Blü World, both from a financial standpoint as well as a growth standpoint. On the Thursday afternoon after we had gotten home, I asked her if she remembered that conversation.

"Yeah," she stated as a faint smile began to grow on her face as she looked up from her computer.

Since Downieville, neither of us had smiled, so I knew this meant something. The first of the two primary goals we had set was simply a certain number in the business bank account she wanted to reach. Back in January, the number I helped her decide on seemed completely unattainable, but I figured it would be a good figure to strive for. Keep in mind, we had picked this number well before we decided to live out of a van for three months, so it did not account for the lull in business that I knew would happen while we were on the road.

Without saying anything else to her, I logged into the business bank account via my phone and couldn't believe what I saw. Not only had she reached her goal and the seemingly unrealistic figure set in January, she had exceeded it. All the while, working out of a van from all across the country.

My jaw dropped as I looked up at her. She was smiling from ear to ear at this point. Then she said, "That's not all..."

The other primary goal was for her to get into an office somewhere in town so that she could begin bringing on a few employees and expanding the business. *Surely, she hadn't already begun to take this on, though.* We had only been back in town for a matter of days. Knowing exactly what I was thinking, she looked down at her computer and made a few clicks on her mouse. Then she slid the screen towards me and told me to look.

On it was a calendar from a realtor's website with numerous dates marked and labeled "Sierra – Blü World." She was already in the process of setting up appointments to check out some office space with a commercial realtor she had met before we had left. This whole time, she had been making huge moves and I didn't even know. That sneaky little grin on her face brought me the first hopeful feelings since tumbling down the rocks in Downieville. I felt inspired.

Sierra often labels me as one of the biggest motivators in her life. Something that we don't often discuss, though, is the motivator she is in my own life. With how big I reach, I tend to fall a lot. The end of that summer, I had fallen hard. Still, Sierra was right there, by my side through it all. Certainly dealing with plenty of her own problems, she continued to help me without question through all of mine. On top of that, she was silently working towards goals and dreams of her own and in magnificent fashion.

The possibility of giving up was gone. I had set out to achieve something, and I wasn't going to stop until it was reached. While I am typically the one motivating and inspiring Sierra to keep going, or to think outside of the box, or to work just a little harder, *it was her turn.* The best part was, she didn't even know she had done it.

All of the premiere events in North America had concluded for the year. The professional mountain bike season was over. With this in mind, I still needed to figure out a way to get myself out there and earn some better support for the following season. I had already decided that it was going to happen; I just needed to figure out *how*.

My mind raced as it often does when I'm in desperate need of a solution. Unfortunately, nothing was coming to me. There was a small regional race, taking place at a ski resort not far from Reno, so I decided to give it a shot in hopes it would maybe spark up a solution in my mind.

While I hadn't ridden since my epic "yard sale" down the mountain at Downieville, I wasn't too concerned about how I finished at this small race. I just wanted to get back into the racing scene and begin to enjoy riding my bike again. Plus, it would be great to hangout with all of my riding friends back on some near-local trails.

I won't get into the specifics of the race that day, as it was fairly uneventful. I ended up winning by a substantial margin, lapping over half of the field. In the process, my ride left quite an impression on one of my competitors, who came up to me after the event.

He introduced himself and explained that he worked for one of the top bicycle manufacturers in the industry in Southern California. He explained that he didn't realize who I was at first, but he recognized the van in the parking lot, as he had seen it in several of our videos and blogs from the summer. It turns out he, and several of his colleagues, had been following the trip closely from back in California.

Since we hadn't blogged or given any updates since we left Vermont, he was curious when I had gotten back into town and wanted to know how the tour ended. As I explained the steady decline since the mechanical issues in Vermont, his face looked shocked as his eyes scanned over my beaten and battered body and torn jersey.

After our conversation, I headed up to the awards ceremony to receive my medal and support the amateur racers who were still finishing up. Later, the same gentleman from before approached me, explaining how he was shocked to see me out racing so soon after the way our tour had concluded.

With Sierra sitting at a table several yards away, talking with friends, I glanced at her before explaining that I just really love racing my bike. You would have to be crazy to go through everything we endured that summer if you didn't absolutely love mountain bike racing. On top of that, I just really believe in the bigger purpose that I see for my life and the first step to getting there is to reach my goals within the sport of cycling.

We chatted for a while, discussing various models of bikes and some of our favorite riding areas in the Sierra Nevada Mountains. As the conversation wound down, there was a short pause as neither of us spoke. Then, it happened.

"So what are your plans for next season?" he asked.

My eyes squinted just slightly as I analyzed the potential implications of the question. "I want to go even bigger," I said confidently.

Looking me in the eye, he just smiled and handed me his card. "Give me a call when you get home. I have some ideas," he said before shaking my hand and walking back towards the parking lot.

Let's Go Ride - Trevor

Perhaps the most difficult chapter of this book to write is this, what you are reading right now. How do you conclude a story that is just beginning? The answer, I've decided, is that you can't.

After that final race just outside of Reno, my lucky connection with the man from the undisclosed bicycle company led to the formation of a humble yet adequate program for me to race the entire Pro XCT series, National Championships, the North American World Cups, and a few international events in the following season.

Sierra has since started her final year of college at the University of Nevada, Reno, where she is probably the only student in any of her classes with their own business, office, and soon, employees. Somehow she finds time to continue to help me with all of my personal branding and web/design needs as well.

Perhaps one of the biggest accomplishments since this unforgettable adventure has been the growth and development of my nonprofit corporation, Reno Tahoe Junior Cycling. There was once a time when I was laughed at for wanting to start such a program because it was believed that kids in the Reno-Tahoe area were simply not interested in riding mountain bikes. Now, with the help of my biggest sponsors and supporters, like Reno-Tahoe Audi, the program has exploded in size.

Having the opportunity to work with the next generation of not only riders, but also *dreamers*, is a privilege beyond words. While I love meeting aspiring little racers, I mostly just enjoy promoting the bicycle, and all that it represents.

You see, the world that we live in today is run by cars. While it takes money to buy a car, it's fair to say that they are accessible to everyone. In fact, it's even fair to say that the automobile is the most acceptable form of transportation in our society. They are safe, reliable, fast, and can take you anywhere the road leads.

For many, the smooth and safe confines of the road are all they need. However, the majority of this planet is not accessible via a road. To some, that's just fine. Often times, people simply accept that they cannot wander off the road, so they never even consider such a thing. Regardless of how intriguing or magnetizing the unknown beauty, mystery, and adventure is that awaits beyond the beaten path, we live in a society where such exploration is not natural.

Still, just because something isn't common doesn't mean it's wrong. Every single great moment in history, like the formation of the United States or the invention of electricity, happened because somebody wasn't afraid to go against the grain and think outside of the box.

This is where the bicycle comes in. Even more accessible than a car, everyone has owned or ridden a bicycle at one point in their lives. While it may seem like a car can take you more places, I'm here to tell you it can't. A bicycle can take anyone anywhere. If you're willing to put in the work, a bicycle will take you to the top of the highest peaks all around the globe. When even the most scenic of highways end, and cars must turn around, a bicycle can continue on, discovering and reaching destinations only accessible to the small percentage of the population willing to put their heart and soul into pressing down on the pedals and forgetting about what everyone else is doing.

It's such a simple analogy, but one that is nonexistent in our education systems today. *Go to school, get a job, get married, have children, retire.* This is the message our society screams at young people until they just accept it and give in. But what happens if you don't accept this? What happens if you pursue more than just money? *To Sierra and I, this is what VanLife represents. This is what entrepreneurship represents.*

With this story, Sierra and I hope to inspire a new generation of dreamers. We can't guarantee your pursuit of passion and purpose will be easy, but we can promise you it will be worthwhile. When you pour your heart and soul into something you deeply care about, the outcome is almost trivial. As long as progress, no matter how indiscernible, is being made towards the bigger vision you see for your life, keep fighting. Keep relentlessly turning your vision into reality, no matter how ridiculous or unobtainable it may seem.

Curious who that undisclosed bike company was that Trevor signed with? Want to see where Trevor and Sierra are today and what their new adventures consist of? Check it all out on ProjectVanLife.com *and stay inspired.*

Acknowledgements

This book and the life I'm living today would not be possible without the support and encouragement of so many. I would like to thank Mark Trujillo for showing me, firsthand, how to build an enterprise out of your passion. Don Pattalock for teaching me how to be a leader and for believing in my racing. I would like to thank Kyle Dixon for helping me fall in love with mountain biking. Sierra Davies for always sticking by my side. And last but not least, I'd like to thank my parents for everything. My life today would not be possible if it wasn't for your love, support, and sacrificed bicycles.
- Trevor

I have so much thanks to give for those who have helped me make it so far. To my parents and brother; your love, support, and encouragement will never go unnoticed or unappreciated. I also want to thank Alice and Liz Heiman for selflessly teaching and guiding me along my journey to becoming a strong, successful, female entrepreneur. And Trevor, thank you for always believing in and inspiring me.
- Sierra

Our sincerest gratitude goes to Dagmar Bohlmann, Sandi Christman, Kevin Joell, Andre Meintjes, and Briana Manning for reading, editing, and helping this book take shape.

Finally, we would like to dedicate Project VanLife to the very first roster of the Reno Tahoe Junior Cycling Race Development Team. Aubrey, Austin, Ian, Jackson, Matt, Preston, Tate, Zach – The world is yours. From cycling and beyond, follow your dreams.

17128675R00150

Made in the USA
San Bernardino, CA
02 December 2014